To Rica

My truly good
friend & brother
Much love

from

Aubrey Morris

Be blessed!

The
POWER
OF
Dreams

The POWER *Of* Dreams

Fuelling Your Purpose & Destiny

AUBREY MORRIS

Printed in the United States of America
ISBN 978-1-64133-681-9 (sc)
ISBN 978-1-64133-682-6 (hc)
ISBN 978-1-64133-683-3 (e)

Library of Congress Control Number: 2021924403

2022.04.16

MainSpring Books
5901 W. Century Blvd
Suite 750
Los Angeles, CA, US, 90045

www.mainspringbooks.com

Author photo by: Paula Kavanagh

TABLE OF CONTENTS

DEDICATION

To my sons Dillon and Levi: dream now and dream big. Let nothing get in your way. Be all that God designed you to be.

To every living human being, I dedicate this book to you also. Be inspired. Be a dreamer!

ACKNOWLEDGEMENTS

Thank you to God my Creator, for the gift of writing. You are the reason I dream.

Thank you to Paula Kavanagh for the author photo.

Thank you to Richard Beeson, Dana Holloman, Reverend Collin Govender and Brendan Marrett for your endorsement of my book. I am truly honoured.

Thank you to Ricardo Erasmus (Life coach, mentor and founder of Paradigm Shift Academy) for your contribution to my chapter on "Flying Without Wings")

Thank you to my Editor: Brendan Marrett for your skilful, literary work.

Thank you to my publisher: Mainsprings Books for working with me in bringing this book to a finished product. Special thanks to: Amber Lopez, my publishing strategist; and Madysson Williams, my book project coordinator; and the rest of the production team at Mainsprings Books.

Thank you to my family and friends for standing with me and believing in my dreams.

Last, but not least, thank you to Auriel, my beautiful wife, for your love, wisdom, courage and support. You are priceless.

FOREWORD

"Dreams by nature are an encouragement and reminder of future possibilities."

The POWER of DREAMS (authored by Aubrey) is the sine qua non for every person in need of a catapult into their purpose and destiny. This book proves to bring a refreshing outlook to life and provides the stimulus and the proverbial defibrillation to the otherwise static soul. It provides a gentle reminder that regardless of whatever point one is in life, that one should never stop dreaming and believing in oneself.

Morris provides his readership with practical insight for daily living. It excites me to have known the author, having grown up in poverty, social injustice and a system that was oppressive, yet he has remarkably endeavoured to break stereotypes by dreaming beyond present prevailing circumstances. Morris resolutely affirms that you can dream big and break beyond every limiting and confining situation. *A must read for every dreamer*!

-Reverend Collin Govender (B. Th. BA Hons. North West University, S.A). Senior Minister—Church on the Move, South Africa, & Secretary of National Mission Board.

Inspirational, informative and motivational are the first three words that come to mind when reading this book. Aubrey has done an excellent job explaining what it means to dream— and dream limitlessly. He has provided enough motivation and practical instruction for you to dispel fear and make your dreams a reality. God is a big God; well able to do exceedingly above all we can ask or dream. I highly recommend this book, especially to those looking to gain a better understanding about dreams, or those who have given up on their dreams. In the words of Aubrey, 'Take your dreams off the shelf', and dream on.

-Dana Holloman (Former Director and Founder of WakeUp Ireland Youth Organization and Church of God Youth Director, Ireland).

Aubrey and I first met in our second year at university in 1994. The passion and love he had for Jesus and his joy in talking about Him at every opportunity was immediately evident. We spent many nights in prayer, worship and theological discussions. The knowledge Aubrey has shared in *The Power of Dreams* will not only add arrows to your quiver, but also sharpen those that are already there. He has provided us with not only an understanding of the types of dreams, but how to value, nurture and action them. The personal stories he has shared provide context and allows you to see more of the man I call friend and brother. Through his book, I have been challenged to dream big, place them before God, and watch, as they become reality. I am certainly looking forward to the next adventure. Are you?

Richard Beeson (Educator: Head teacher, England).

In this disquisition of dreams, Aubrey surveys: their divine origin; their purpose and role in our everyday lives as well as our future; how to nurture these promises of God; how to reclaim our confidence in our dreams when they have been knocked, torn asunder, or their materialization appears impossible; and how to wisely operate as part of a corporate body to bring our dreams to fulfilment. This is an essential asset to those navigating the voyage from living as a dreamer to living the dream.

Brendan Marrett (Educator: Masters Degree in English Language and Teaching Skills)

PREFACE

DREAMS are an integral part of human existence. They are crucial to your life's journey, to your future, to your destiny. They serve as a cursor that assists in manoeuvring you in the direction you desire to go.

Do you have a vision for your life? What are you envisioning? What are some of your targets? What are you picturing regarding your future? Are you working towards some goals because of your dreams?

God gives dreams that propel you towards the destiny He has set for you. Dreams are exciting; even more so when they materialize or become a reality. Dreams are like that special window that allows you a glimpse into your future. Do not ignore that special window. Your future is a very important factor in your life. It is more important than your past and your present.

Best-selling author and founder of the Bahamas Faith Ministries International Organisation Doctor Myles Munroe once wrote, *"The poorest person in the world is a person without a dream (idea; vision)."* He then went on to write, *"The most frustrated person in the world is someone who has a dream, but doesn't know how to make it come to pass."*

Thirdly, he wrote, *"God has placed in every human being a unique vision and call that is designed to give purpose and meaning to life. Every person was created to be known for something special."*

If you do not tap into what is inside you, you will never know your richness or enjoy it. You will be aimless and unfruitful in this regard.

Are you a BIG DREAMER? Do you love dreaming? Do you love new ideas and inventions? It is wonderful to receive new things. You should be excited about new dreams and new ideas, and setting new goals. The beginning of every day, week, month or year brings fresh starts and fresh opportunities. This keeps you hopeful. It keeps you active, energized and progressive, knowing you can invest your life into something new and life-changing. It keeps the cogwheels of purpose and destiny turning.

Your life should have a certain amount of momentum to it. You will stumble into a rut of stagnation without dreams. Dreaming is like riding a bicycle. As long as you keep riding, you will not fall off. The key is to keep your dream cycle moving so you do not fall away from pursuing purpose and destiny. If you feel like you are stagnating, then you need to stir up those dreams with action, and with momentum.

Some people are afraid of their dreams, especially when those dreams are huge with the possibility of an epic reach. More often than not, dreams will be bigger than your present reality. Just because your conditions may be adverse to your dreams, does not mean your dreams will not happen. Never shelve your dreams due to challenging and unsavoury circumstances, for to do so is as good as shelving your purpose and success, since they are all inextricably linked. If you desire success, then regardless of external or internal challenges, you will have to take your dreams off the shelf and pursue them.

Remember, circumstances are subject to change. They do not have to stop the nurturing and fulfilment of your dreams. Treat your dreams like seeds. You may not be able to plant your type of seeds in winter, but winter does not last forever. Spring will come when you can plant your dreams and grow them, and see a harvest in your summer. Having a future guarantees not only that you will experience change, but also that you are going to have a chance to exhibit your potential. The world wants to know what you possess and what you are all about. Your Maker uniquely designed you to affect the world and those around you in a significant and positive way. Understand that you and your dreams are a benefit to society.

With that said, thoughtfulness, focus, and action are required on your part, and oftentimes, a daunting amount of each. Dreams cannot fulfil themselves. Dreaming is one thing, but bringing those dreams to life or reality is quite another. The rewards though are deeply satisfying and beneficial.

Dreams will require much effort and preparation. They will require your focus and time. You have to keep your eye on the ball, so to speak, or else you will not score in life. Stay focused on your dreams and goals, and let all opposing distractions remain on the periphery.

You cannot afford to be a lone ranger on planet earth. Your dreams will require the effort of others alongside you, to help you fulfil them. That is why God blesses you with family, friends, acquaintances, coaches, teachers, motivational speakers, advisers and others. They are there to lend some assistance in bringing your dreams to life. However, it is still your responsibility to own your dreams and purposefully pursue them. Nobody can dream your dreams and live them out better than you can. People who leave their dreams dormant, or who are careless with their dreams, end up taking many of those powerful dreams to the grave. Make your mark on earth, not in the grave where earthly potential ceases.

Disallowing the grave from claiming them, I desire to fulfil as many of my dreams as possible. In addition, when the inevitable challenges and obstacles arise, I will press on with determination, patience and willpower. Success is not always easy, but it is possible.

No one said life would be a bed of roses; but it does not have to be a complete bed of thorns either. You can enjoy your dreams and the journey they take you on. You can enjoy your life. Dreams concerning your purpose and destiny should affect you positively. Surround your dreams with positivity and optimism. Be excited about your dreams. Do not allow a pessimistic attitude, or pessimistic people, for that matter, to diffuse your passion for your dreams.

What do your dreams look like? What are you doing with them? What are you doing to stay motivated and passionate about them? Where are you drawing strength and courage from regarding your dreams? Well, this book will fuel your passion about bringing dreams to life. For those who have buried their dreams, either because of insecurity, limitations or fear; it is time to realise and resurrect those dreams. It is time to discard those fears, and discard negativity and insecurity.

For those of you, who think it is too late for that dream burning in your heart to happen, let me say, it is never too late to dream. Whether you are old or young, you can still bring your dreams to fulfilment. Let me stir up those dreams in your heart. Let this book be the fire that sets alight those cold and dying dreams you once were passionate about. See how your dreams can bring you to a great destiny, while serving as a catalyst that propels others forward in the fulfilment of their dreams.

For those of you who have fulfilled your dreams, and feel there is nothing more or greater for you to accomplish; I say dig a little deeper. There is more in you. See yourself as a 'well that never runs dry'. As long as you are alive, never stop dreaming. As long as there is breath in you, remain boundless, incessant, and unstoppable. As renowned theologian and author Clive Staples Lewis said, *"You are never too old to set another goal or to dream a new dream."*

GO CONFIDENTLY IN
THE DIRECTION OF YOUR
DREAMS! LIVE THE LIFE
YOU'VE IMAGINED.

- Thoreau

CHAPTER 1

UNDERSTANDING DREAMS

By basic definition, a dream is a *series of thoughts, images and sensations occurring in a person's mind, usually during sleep.* Obviously, this does not suggest that dreaming cannot happen at other times; we know that a person can experience a dream, whether asleep or awake.

Another definition of a dream is **"vision of the night"** (Job 33:15, NKJV).

The thrust of this book is about your dreams relating to your purpose for life. The things you are passionate about and desire to achieve. The particular career path you desire to follow. Sometimes there may be more than one path. Your dreams help form your vision for life, out of which flow hope, inspiration and your great contribution to the world. Your dreams ultimately lead to you achieving your purpose, through which your potential is exercised and maximised. You have to become ambitious about your dreams; meaning you are willing to do something to fulfil them. Dreams reveal a lot about what is happening in a person's mind and life.

Do not ignore your dreams. Be passionate about them. In the same breath, you should not become fanatic or overly obsessed with dreams. Developing a healthy and balanced approach to your dreams is the best thing to do.

Dreams may seem intangible and abstract to others, and even to you. However, if you work on them, you can transform them into something tangible and concrete. Dreams require an element of faith, because they cause you to wander paths you have never walked before, and inspire you to pluck from the realm of invisibility and translate it into the tangible and visible. Dreams start in the heart, and then, require an outward expression, and not just remain internalized.

There are times when people experience or see things, which may play out in their dreams. The reverse can also happen, where one dreams of a thing, not previously experienced, that then becomes a reality. For instance, someone could dream of going into labour, and then the next day birth a new project. Again, a man may dream of meeting a woman he does not know, and the next day or near future, meet someone new, or begin a new relationship. Then at some point in the future, they could end up a married couple. Thirdly, a teacher might dream of being attacked at work, and the next day or week, an unruly student amasses against him or her. Even if you are not sure of the origin of the dream, at least seek to uncover its meaning.

People are not estranged to dreaming. People have been having dreams for thousands of years before our time. A dream is designed to inspire, warn, remind, foretell (predict; prophesy), point to, or reveal something. Do bear in mind, my primary focus is on the power dreams have in the fulfilment of your purpose and destiny, as opposed to the interpretation of nocturnal visions. Most of your dreams have a bearing on your destiny. Understanding your dreams and the times and seasons of your life is crucial to reaching your destiny.

Futuristic in nature, dreams enable the dreamer to transcend the present moment. They all happen in your heart and in your mind. Then you have the job of working them out in your life practically. As I have said previously, it is all about externalizing the internal. A beautiful flower was once a seed, with all that beauty confined in the seed. Once planted, that seed began to release that built-in ability to produce that beautiful flower. Your dreams are like seeds. Plant them and see them develop and bring out your greatness. At some point, you have to birth what you have been carrying ("pregnant" with) inside. Bear in mind that the realization of your dreams is there to benefit others, not just yourself. Dreams can be external too. God might give you a dream that has nothing to do with you, but is entirely for someone else.

God wants you and me to understand dreams and visions. The Bible tells us that dreams and interpretations belong to God (Genesis 40:8). Daniel was able to understand visions and dreams because God enabled him to. The book of Daniel details this account:

"As for these four young men, God gave them knowledge and skill in all literature and wisdom; and understanding in all visions and dreams" (Daniel 1:17, NKJV).

Bear in mind that as much as dreams can be interpreted correctly, it is also possible to interpret them incorrectly. Therefore, wisdom and caution—and above all, God's guidance—are required.

TYPES OF DREAMS

Dreams are oftentimes an enigmatic, arbitrary means of discourse through which God communes with people. It is important to note that the succeeding explanations will not apply to every such dream.

1. **A Daydream:** This is one of the most common kinds of dreams. By definition, a daydream is a *visual fantasy occurring while you are awake; where your brain engages over important or exciting issues that are not immediately relevant.* Normally, pleasant daydreams cultivate within the dreamer a positive frame of mind, allowing him or her to envisage their future goals and aspirations. Day dreaming should not be viewed as something negative whether it happens to adults or children. When you cannot yet live out a reality in the *now*, you can at least dream of it in the *now*.

2. **Warning Dreams:** These types of dreams may warn of impending danger. One example is when an angel warned Joseph in a dream to take Jesus and flee to Egypt because King Herod wanted to kill the child. He wanted to eliminate the competition to his title and legacy:

   ". . . an angel of the Lord appeared to Joseph in a dream, saying, 'Arise, and take the young child [Jesus] and mother [Mary], flee into Egypt, and stay there until I bring you word; for Herod will seek the young child to destroy [kill] him'" (Matthew 2:13, NKJV).

God then similarly employed dreams as His mechanism by which to warn the Magi, or Wise Men, not to tell Herod where Jesus was, since, in his carnal understanding, the fretful king suspected that the child would usurp him:

"Then, being divinely warned in a dream that they [Wise men] should not return to Herod, they departed for their own country another way" (Matthew 2:12, NKJV).

Personally, I have had dreams where God warned me of some things. I was then able to do certain things in my life to counteract that. I also recall a dream God gave me about someone. This dream came as a warning to a potentially negative future situation. I shared the dream with the person concerned. They did not heed the warning and suffered the consequences. There were several other warning dreams I have had where I was able to warn those concerned. They heeded the warning and thereby did not suffer the negative consequences. Obviously, one does not need to become paranoid about every single dream of this sort, however, it is good to note those dreams that alarm you or tug at your heart in some way.

3. **Prophetic (Predictive) Dreams:** These relate to the future. It is not always easy to determine whether this kind of dream is prophetic until it actually happens. Prophetic dreams are spiritual. God speaks to people about the future in this way. A reference for this is in the Bible book of Job 33:14-15. It says, *". . . God always answers, one way or another, even when people don't recognize his presence. In a dream, for instance, a vision of the night, when men and women are deep in sleep, fast asleep in their beds—God opens their ears and impresses [instructs] them with warnings to turn them back from something bad they're planning, from some reckless choice . . ."* (MSG.)

God is able to speak to you because you are a spirit, possessing a soul and living in a physical body (1 Thessalonians 5:23). You should endeavour to unravel the symbolisms and mysteries revealed in these prophetic dreams. Seek God's guidance, and pray about the messages He relays to you.

In Genesis, chapter 37, Joseph, a young Canaanite man, had two prophetic dreams that pointed to his future and destiny. At some point, in the future, both dreams came to pass. While he was imprisoned in the dungeons of Egypt under false charges, Joseph also interpreted the enigmatic dreams of the butler and the baker. These two dreams materialized exactly as he had said they would, which proved celebratory for the butler, but less so for the death-row-bound baker.

Fast forward two years to the seminal night when God told Pharaoh of a future event he had to prepare for—a time of great blessing followed by a terrible upheaval or famine— but Pharaoh could not humanly discern the meaning of the two dreams. Both of the king's dreams pointed to the same thing—a seven-year period where there would be plenty of grain and provisions. The second part of the dreams pointed to a severe famine that would ravage the land of Egypt and some other countries for a seven-year period. Under Joseph's guidance Egypt accumulated unfathomable surplus provisions of food and grain during the years of plenty. Hence, the understanding of the dreams sustained and saved many lives during the seven-year famine.

In the Bible book of Daniel, King Nebuchadnezzar summoned Daniel to interpret his dreams. Daniel revealed to the king that God had enabled him to interpret dreams. Then Daniel went ahead and told the king what his dreams were signifying. This is found in the book of Daniel, chapter 2.

4. **A Nightmare:** A nightmare is not the kind of dream you want to have. Classed as a bad dream; this is related to some terrible or traumatic occurrence and evokes feelings of fear and distress. It is called Post-Traumatic Stress Nightmare (PSN). For example, someone who has been through a bad accident or terror attack or physical abuse, may wake up in fear and stress from their mind reliving the experience while asleep.

   The second kind of nightmare occurs where people have watched something terrifying, like a horror movie or terrifying computer game. These play back in some horror form as a dream, resulting in the person experiencing emotional and mental upset and fear. Personally, this is an unnecessary self-inflicted problem. Stop these nightmares by abstaining from such movies, games, or visual apparatus.

   According to doctors, some medications can trigger nightmares. These are brought on by certain drugs that act on chemicals in the brain, such as antidepressants and narcotics. Nightmares can happen to children and adults. The relief often comes after one realises the nightmare was not real.

   The Bible book of Ecclesiastes says that God gives his children peaceful sleep; meaning, He is not the source of people's nightmares. Rather, God wants you to experience pleasant dreams. One ought to confront and deal with nightmares. Getting to the root of the problem can bring a resolution and relief.

5. **Open Vision:** This kind of visual encounter happens when a person's physical senses are suspended and another realm opens up to them, where they can see into another dimension or spiritual world. This happened to a believer by the name of

Stephen. This took place just before the angry mob could stone him to death for simply preaching the Gospel of Jesus.

"But he [Stephen], being full of the Holy Spirit, gazed into Heaven and saw the glory of God, and Jesus standing at the right hand of God, and said, 'Look! I see the heavens opened and the Son of Man [Jesus Christ] standing at the right hand of God!'" (Acts 7:55-56, NKJV).

Here, Stephen was amazed with what he saw. The others around him did not see what he saw, for the vision was closed to them. They must have thought Stephen had lost his mind, because when they looked up they only saw clouds and sky.

6. **Guiding Dream:** This kind of dream or vision serves to enlighten or guide an individual towards an answer or destination. It gives direction or illumination. For example, God used this kind of dream to help a certain devout Roman Centurion called Cornelius and his family. One afternoon, Cornelius had a vision in which he saw an angel of God. The angel gave him instructions, after commending him for his generosity and prayers. The angel told him to send men to a place called Joppa to invite Simon Peter to his house. God was going to use Simon Peter to share the Gospel of salvation with Cornelius and his family.

While this was happening, God gave Peter a vision where he fell into a trance. God asked Peter to eat that which Jews considered forbidden. This vision was not really about food. Rather, it was God getting Peter to change his mind-set about associating with Gentiles. God was preparing him to take the Gospel of salvation to Cornelius, a Gentile. Prior to this Peter had only been preaching to the Jews. The enlightenment he received from the vision was that God had opened up salvation to all people, and not just Jewish people. This account is found in the Bible book of Acts, chapter ten.

7. **Dreaming of Death:** This type of dream could symbolise a season in your life, where something is ending or dying out. It could be a relationship, a project, or a career. It can also point to something new coming. Sombrely, it could also point to a physical death of a loved one, or someone trying to come to terms with a recent bereavement.

8. **Dreaming of Flying:** This kind of dream may symbolise a desire to be free. It could symbolise the dreamer's feelings of unrestrained happiness, whether it is a new job, a relationship or great holiday. It can also represent going higher in the things of the Spirit and increased revelation in the things of God.

9. **Dreaming of a Baby:** This dream can reveal one's desire for a physical baby, or it may be confirmation from God that you are going to birth something new and full of life and vitality. This dream can also reveal one's need for care and love, or apparent vulnerability.

10. **Dreaming of Being Chased:** This type of dream could mean that you are threatened by something or someone. You may be trying to distance yourself from some unsavoury situation in real life.

11. **Dreaming of Clothes:** This dream could symbolise the dreamer's desire to make a certain statement about their image, or what image they desire to portray. Shabby clothes may imply he or she feels worn or unattractive, or has a low self-esteem. In stark contrast, good-quality, pristine clothes may demonstrate feelings of attractiveness and confidence. Clothes can also

represent a blessing, or God's anointing and mandate for one's life.

12. **Dreaming of Falling:** This dream could relate to anxiety over letting go of something; or someone losing control over something. It can also be due to someone failing at something in which they once were successful. It could also symbolise someone's once-great, but now tarnished reputation.

13. **Dreaming of Nudity:** Nudity can represent a number of things: a desire to reveal one's true self; feelings of vulnerability; a fear that lifestyle, choices, secrets, or abilities will be exposed; sexual urges; or a desire to be recognized.

14. **Dreaming of Sex:** This type of dream may reveal a need for intimacy, or a desire for a sexual encounter. It may also symbolise the fusion of two great things in a person's life that give rise to something phenomenal. It may also reveal an addiction to something. We are frequently bombarded by sexual banter, sexual images, sexual innuendos and sensual adverts that get buried in the sub-conscience, and later, may seep out into a dream.

15. **Dreaming of Teachers:** This dream may represent people who are in authority and who enlighten others. If it relates to one's career, it could be an indication of someone's desire to be a teacher.

16. **Dreaming of being Trapped:** This dream could show that someone feels trapped in a relationship or job. It could also show someone's anxiety to overcome an addiction in life. It may also point to one's difficulty in trying to get out of a sticky or tricky situation.

17. **Dreaming of Vehicles:** This dream may reflect someone's current control over life and circumstances. It may also reflect one's ability to drive things forward, such as a ministry or business, and the ability to take people on a journey. It may also occur because of an intense desire for a vehicle you really like.

18. **Dreaming of A Mansion:** This dream could symbolise someone's successes and huge opportunities. It could mean that one feels larger than life and unrestricted. It can also point to an actual physical mansion you have or are close to possessing. It can also mean you have something of which you are proud.

19. **Dreaming of Exams:** This dream could mean someone is literally under investigation. It may also be because they have an upcoming exam, or they may be doing a self-evaluation of their own life.

20. **Dreaming of Water:** This dream can symbolise a quenching of a thirst or a need in the dreamer's life, if the person actively participates in the dream and drinks the water. A calm pool or ocean of water may point to the peace and tranquillity in life. Choppy and rough waters may point to uneasiness and turmoil in someone's life. Water can also symbolise influence, as in the Beast out of the Sea in the Bible book of Revelation; the wicked figure who arises from the pool of political figureheads to wage war against the saints. Additionally, water can represent the Holy Spirit, as in Ezekiel's vision where the waters came up from underneath the threshold and saturated the land.

21. **Dreaming of Missing a Flight:** This dream may symbolise someone's frustration over missed opportunities in life. It can also suggest delay in his or her decision-making, where they have missed the right timing or season to execute a task or project, or a needed change.

22. **<u>Dreaming of Teeth:</u>** Dreaming of teeth falling out or crumbling could indicate a difficult transition. It could mean someone is anxious about growing old. It can also point to insecurity concerning huge life changing decisions. The late dream interpreter John-Paul Jackson gave an alternative, though probably equally true explanation: dreams of teeth falling out represent one's ability to chew on or grasp information.

66

**BELIEVE IN YOUR DREAMS.
THEY ARE GIVEN TO
YOU FOR A REASON.**

- Katrina Mayer

CHAPTER 2

BE A DREAMER

Everyone is a dreamer. Dreaming is as natural as breathing. Sometimes we do it without realizing that we are dreaming. From the time we were little, we were dreamers, and whether children or adults, we are still dreamers.

Dreaming is an ability all humans possess, irrespective of colour, language, creed, culture or geographic location. No one is disadvantaged when it comes to dreaming. No one can dream for you. Your dreams are personal and purposeful. What you do with those dreams is entirely up to you. God gives you dreams so that you can catch a glimpse of your future; so you can realize your purpose and destiny. We live forward, not backwards, so dreams are crucial, for they give forward momentum to life. Dreams cause you to focus on your future and grasp new opportunities; whereas regrets keep you bound to your past mistakes and missed opportunities.

One of the reasons for stagnation is the lack of the injection of life and passion into one's dreams. Dormant dreams cannot revive themselves. They are like seeds. You have to do the planting and watering.

Almost everything starts out with a dream; with an idea; with an intuition. Even God is a dreamer. He dreamed of the earth and human beings, and then made those dreams a reality. Simply put, you are God's dream. The Bible tells us that God has a dream to create a new Heaven and new Earth. There is more to come. Dreams let you know that there is more to come.

As long as you are dreaming, there is always more. More is good. It means the end has not come yet. God did not put less in you, but more. God is all about abundance and full potential concerning your life. Take an inward look, and you will be surprised at what you will discover inside you. There is so much more to you than what the eye can see.

A daydream is not a waste of time, as some people profess it to be. It just means the person daydreaming has shifted their focus from the present to something else. They have given their attention to something else. Sometimes people daydream, and do not even realise it, until they are snapped out of that detachment from their immediate surroundings and reality.

Many years ago, as a young boy sitting in class, my mind would wander into my near future. I would dream of things. I would design and plan things in my mind. I would think of things I wanted to make. I would think of the kind of career I wanted, or the kind of woman I wanted to marry, or the kind of car I wanted to drive. Then the teacher would snap me out my daydream. Teachers discouraged daydreaming. They chalked it off as not paying attention or not being focused. True enough, I was not focused on the present task; but nonetheless, I was focused on something else—MY FUTURE; MY ASPIRATIONS. Kids are big dreamers. Do you remember when you were a kid? Do you remember how curious and adventurous your mind was? Hopefully, you have not lost that spark if you are in your mature years. Keep a creative mind and an adventurous spirit. You really do not have time to shelve your dreams, especially if you are in your latter years. Make things happen. Cast off fear and apathy. Get busy; get creative; exert your potential.

People get old, but dreaming does not get old. Creativity does not age, or wear out. You do not have to worry, for you will never run out of dreams and creativity. You will run out of youth; out of strength; out of time, but not out of dreams. The living should be dreaming most of the time. There should be a flow of dreams in your life. Olympic victor and multiple-times world heavyweight champion "Big George" Foreman made an interesting statement. He said, *"If you don't dream you might as well be dead."* This speaks to the life, love and excitement of dreams. Imagine how boring life would be if you had nothing to build, create or look forward to.

Many men and women have dreamed and built things that have lasted beyond their lifespan. Have you ever walked passed a store or some business that had the name Father and Son; or Established 1820, and is still existing through a grandson or granddaughter. This is a good thing, to have your dreams outlive you. That is part of your legacy. You and I still benefit from the dreams of people who are no longer living.

Do you remember all the dreams you had in your youth? As you got older, your dreams grew. You discovered more things about yourself and your inner desires. Your hunger for the unknown grew. Your hunger for adventure heightened. Your zest for life fuelled your dreams. Your dreams will keep alive that spark in your heart and in your eyes. If you are not dreaming, you have nothing to hang your future on.

Dreams are vehicles that propel you into your future. They create momentum in your life. Dreaming keeps things fresh in your life. Do not allow yourself to stagnate because of the dormancy of your dreams and vision. Apathy is the enemy of true progression.

Sometimes I say it out loudly: "I AM A DREAMER." Then I must go a step further and say, "I AM A DOER OF MY DREAMS!" Are you a doer of your dreams? It is pointless being a dreamer, and not having the desire to convert those dreams into reality. Having good ideas and thoughts is good. Putting those thoughts and ideas into action is even better.

As I have said before, dreams move you into your purpose and destiny. Joseph accomplished his purpose as the Prime Minister of Egypt by following his dreams, even when he experienced difficulty. Behind the scenes, God was orchestrating things to bring Joseph to a point of destiny. God will use your dreams to bring you to your destiny. Difficulty and obstacles can be signs that your dreams are great and worth pursuing. Dig deeper, press harder. Stay the course. It is worth the sacrifice. Success (winning) is not always easy, but it is always possible. Learn to celebrate your wins and bounce back from your setbacks. Remain buoyant.

No one should run out of dreams. God gives us plenty of them. It is not so much about the dreams you have at night, but the ones in your heart. They are all tied to your purpose and destiny. Those dreams you long to fulfil; dreams that cause you to stay awake late at night, excited and expectant of great things to come. If your life is boring, you probably are not working on your dreams.

The Wright brothers were dreamers. They dreamed of flying. Their first invention of an aeroplane was somewhat insignificant. Nevertheless, twelve seconds in the air was better than zero seconds in the air. That small start was a glimpse of something great. Simply put, we must never despise small beginnings. A tall oak tree was once a small acorn seed. Those twelve seconds in the air by the Wright Brothers provided them with fuel and excitement to press ahead. Today we all benefit from their dream. I quite enjoy flying, thanks to the Wright brothers. So what dreams are in your heart? Perhaps your next dream could revolutionize the world in some great way. For example, think of the founders of Facebook or Instagram. Their dream to build these social media platforms started small but made giant leaps and revolutionized how we engage social media platforms.

Do not underestimate your dreams. Place a high value on them. It does not matter how small the start. Only small-minded people will belittle it. Great minds look beyond the small start and see a grand finish.

Having dreams is one thing, but believing in them is quite another. Then there is that decision to pursue and fulfil those dreams. People who have no intention of fulfilling their dreams defeat the purpose of those dreams. To reiterate, dreams should not be taken to the grave, nor be put on a shelf. They are given for this life. God would have never allowed you to dream if there was no purpose attached to those dreams.

If you do not unveil and work towards your dreams and goals, others will use you or employ you to fulfil their dreams and vision. I am not saying you cannot help others or work for others, especially if you know you are called to do that. However, if you have a burning desire to fulfil a dream in your heart, then do it. Otherwise, you will become frustrated and discouraged. Do not expend all your energy and years on things that take you away from your dreams.

If all you do is dream throughout your life, with no steps or action towards fulfilling those dreams, then you will be labelled a dreamer in a negative sense. Being a dreamer is closely linked to your imagination and creativity. However, this should lead to a practical or a viable outworking of those dreams. Imagine if God only dreamed of creating us humans, or the entire planet for that matter. Everything would have existed only in God's mind or imagination. You are not just a dreamer or a thinker; but you must be a doer. God did something about what He envisioned. He got practical about it. Get practical with your dreams. In the words of T.D. Jakes: "Work that thing".

You should not just encourage others to dream. You should not just help others fulfil their dreams. You should not just celebrate the achievements of others while ignoring your dreams. You must get others to help you. The help you distribute to others ought to be reciprocated. When you sow something good, you want to reap something good.

Human beings have much in common. They desire greatness. They desire success. They all dream of future achievements. This means there will always be others to encourage you to keep dreaming. They will provide a roadmap for where you want to go; especially those who have walked a similar path to the one you are walking. If you cannot find trailblazers, then blaze the trail yourself. You become that roadmap that will also help others forward. Become that spark that inspires others. Ignite the dreams of others. Light up someone's life. I love to help and see people fulfil their dreams. That is why I wrote this book.

As a dreamer, you must remain expectant. You must convince yourself that your dreams can become a reality. This makes it fun, instead of daunting. You get to realize the possibilities more than the impossibilities and obstacles. Excitement for your dreams should outweigh difficulties or challenges that come as a result of you pressing into your dreams.

You must have confidence in your ability to accomplish what you dream. Do not be overwhelmed with the enormity of your dreams. Remember, the man who has walked a thousand steps began with one single step. Focus on that first step, then the next. After some time, when you look back, you will be amazed with the many steps you have achieved.

The Hallmark of True Dreamers:

> ➢ Dreamers make plans, not just predictions or half-baked statements.
> ➢ Dreamers possess inspiration and motivation.

➢ Dreamers invent, imagine, and create, instead of re-hashing the same old formulae as previous generations.

➢ Dreamers have a strong desire to see their goals accomplished, and determination to see their goals through to completion.

➢ Dreamers are patient and operate with precision.

➢ Dreamers acquire facts and truth, not just opinions.

➢ Dreamers are trailblazers, and aim to set new records.

➢ Dreamers find a way, not an excuse.

➢ Dreamers change lives and circumstances.

➢ Dreamers are willing to make huge sacrifices to see their dreams fulfilled.

My encouragement to you is for you to KEEP DREAMING. This is where greatness begins. This is the birthing place of greatness. This is the place where circumstances change for the good. This is the place where God meets you and reveals to you your mandate or commission. You were born to dream. You are empowered to dream. Write your story.

ALL OUR DREAMS CAN
COME TRUE, IF WE
HAVE THE COURAGE
TO PURSUE THEM.

- Walt Disney

CHAPTER 3

NURTURING YOUR DREAMS

When I consider this subject of nurturing one's dreams, I tend to think of a mother with her new-born baby. She is fully aware she is carrying in her arms a precious gift; one that needs time, attention, dedication and providence. A baby is a great gift, but also a great responsibility. For many years onward, parents will give their time, attention, resources, energy and love to support that baby. These things cause the baby to grow into a fully functioning and balanced man or woman. That is the goal of their 'dream baby,' so to speak.

Your dreams are quite similar, in that they will require your time, patience, passion, energy, and other sacrifices to bring them to fulfilment. It is not just about having dreams, but also being responsible with them. It is about bringing them to full maturity. If a fruit tree had a dream, it would be about bringing its fruit to maturity. It would take in all required nutrients, sunlight and water in order to grow and ripen its fruit. Failing to produce and mature its fruit equals unfulfilled purpose. Do not fail to recognize and capitalize on the power of your dreams. The fulfilment of your dreams is the fulfilment of purpose. Dormant or neglected dreams lead to unfulfilled purpose.

Whether you are at the beginning or middle of a dream you are working on, it will still require nurturing. You cannot just abandon your dreams. Your dreams will not fulfil themselves. That job is reserved for you, the dreamer. Neither does it make any sense to give your dreams to someone else. Your dreams are for you to fulfil. The passion has to come from you. Your dreams are unique to you.

What are you nurturing? Some people have become skilled in nurturing the wrong things; like bitterness, hate, revenge, hurt and un-forgiveness. These will never produce a full and healthy life. They are hindrances to one's progress or forward momentum. When there are new and elevating things to pursue, then you have to let go of the old and burnt out things. Let go of those things that keep you from soaring higher. A wet blanket is put over a fire to put it out. However, if you want that fire to burn, remove the wet blanket. Give that fire oxygen. Give your dreams oxygen. Give them focus, energy and resources. Speak positively over your dreams. Let them live and grow.

People who hold on to things that they are supposed to let go of, probably do not believe there is anything else greater for them. God will not prompt you to give something up without having something else set up for you that outshines the previous thing. Do your best to nurture those things that will benefit you and others.

Avoid nurturing things that will not profit you. It matters greatly what you do with your resources, energy and time.

Avoid wasting your time and energy on things that do not yield profit or fruitfulness. You only have one life—Make it count.

You have to feed or fuel your dreams. Plants need good soil, sunlight and water in order to grow well. Discover those things that will cause your dreams to grow. Those things need to be positive things. You need things like passion, joy, patience, optimism, belief, faith, knowledge, temperance and strategy. You must not leave your dreams undernourished. Malnourished dreams cannot catapult you into your grand destiny. Malnourished dreams will not give you the buoyancy and optimism you need.

Dreams have the ability to keep you afloat even in adverse circumstances. You could have nothing else going for you, except a dream. That dream still keeps you hopeful and expectant. Nelson Mandela is a true example of a man who did not let go of his dream for a democratic and free South Africa even while confined in a prison cell on Robben Island.

Right Attitude

It is often said that attitude affects everything. It is also said that attitude affects or determines altitude. Your attitude determines how high or how far you go in life. Attitude is about how you think, feel, perceive and behave towards people or things. A bad attitude can be like throwing water on a fire that is supposed to keep you warm. It is like trying to drive a vehicle with a flat tyre. Some people cut off their own success by their bad attitude towards others, or their dreams, or just life in general. God did not give you life for you to be careless or frivolous with it. If you discover you have a bad attitude, do not lose all hope. A bad attitude is changeable. It needs to be treated, just as a flat tyre needs repairing for any further momentum.

Your dreams will require the help and skills of other people. You can push people away with a bad attitude. This is not beneficial, for you need others when it comes to fulfilling your dreams. It is easier to get help when you are likable and cordial. Understand that your tone and attitude is what people 'feel,' oftentimes more than what you actually say. Attitude may be seen as a small thing, but it makes a huge difference. Pastor of the Potter's House (Dallas, Texas), T.D. Jakes said, *"If you are to achieve the dreams set before you, it will require a team effort, with many supporting players."* Therefore, do not alienate the people God has placed alongside you over something as careless and treatable as a bad attitude or foul temper.

You will need wisdom and an attitude that draws supporters in and keeps them motivated and committed to helping you bring your dreams to pass. Learn to cherish those people who are entirely committed to the dream or course you are working on. One of the ways to cherish and appreciate them is by having a pleasant attitude towards them. No one really enjoys working with difficult people.

Attitude is not limited to people only. You have to have the right attitude towards all areas and factors of your life. One's attitude towards one's day is vital. All you have are days; and you can only live one day at a time. You must realize that each day leads to the culmination of your dreams. Are you doing the right things in your day to push those dreams ahead? If you waste your days, you actually end up wasting your week, month, and even your year. You end up wasting opportunities to propel your dreams forward.

A day can present you with many opportunities. What is your attitude or outlook towards the day you have? I came across this quote by Kerrie Anne Boyce, a friend of mine, while on Instagram: "RISE UP AND ATTACK EACH DAY WITH ENTHUSIASM." This is simple, but profound. You must channel your energy, resources and focus in a way that impacts your day favourably. It is living that day to the fullest. It is about enjoying that next step that brings you closer to the reality of your dreams. You must keep a winning attitude even when faced with difficulties in your path. A winning attitude says, 'No matter how low I go, I will eventually rise to the top.'

Some people only think in terms of the week, month or year. Whether you have short or long-term goals, each day matters. You do not want unfruitful days, which can lead to an unfruitful week, month or year. You do not want to look back over the course of your life and realise you have left no significant mark. Your generation needs you and the dreams you have. You are here to make a difference. Dreams make a difference.

It is emotionally and spiritually rewarding to begin and end your day with prayer. It helps to pray about things that matter to you. This causes you to realise your need for God and His divine guidance regarding all aspects of life. You get to commit the day ahead, allowing the hand of God to mould, fashion, change and reposition you according to His plan and purpose for your life. Many times God will use other people and even circumstances to achieve the recalibrations you require. No human being is self-made, but God-made. He wants to help you nurture your life and your dreams.

A 'self-made' attitude will soon wear a person out. This life is not designed for a person to walk alone, nor fulfil dreams and goals in his or her own strength. Don't try to be a lone ranger. God and other people are central to the fulfilling of your dreams. Do not repel them, but welcome them as helpers, advisers, coaches, friends and partners. You will require certain trustworthy and wise people to keep you accountable, motivated, determined and grounded.

Having a good or positive attitude has many benefits. I have mentioned some of them already. There is a resilience and confidence when you have a positive attitude. You can face challenges with optimism. Optimism is the cure for a pessimistic attitude. Having a positive outlook and attitude keeps you hopeful in despairing circumstances. You cope better with the affairs of daily life with a positive attitude. Obstacles become easier to overcome with a positive attitude. We tend to talk to ourselves often, if not verbal, at least in thought. Constant negative self-talk will rob you of positive progression. Talk yourself into victory, and not defeat.

Right Mind-set

Your mind is crucial to your achievements, and crucial to your well-being. What you think and say does affect your life largely. Your mind is driven primarily by what grabs your attention, your mind and your heart.

A wise proverb says:

"For as he thinks in his heart, so is he . . ."
(Proverbs 23:7, NKJV).

Mind-set has to do with thought processes, reasoning and perception. The Oxford Dictionary defines mind-set as a *"fixed mental attitude or disposition that predetermines a person's responses to and interpretation of situations."* People react or respond a certain way to things because their mind has been conditioned, wired or trained that way. If you desire to change your reaction or response to something, then first change your mind-set. You do this by the vigorous repetition of something new or different to counter-act the old.

Many things you say or do start out as a thought. Speaking is like thinking out aloud. Not everything you think will be wholesome. Those are the thoughts you need to discard, but you ought to water and cultivate the good ones. They are like seeds with the potential to produce something. Bad seeds cannot produce a good harvest. Similarly, bad or negative thinking hardly leads to a wholesome life, and to wholesome success. Be aware of what you are sowing, be it in word or deed.

There is this famous saying that *your thoughts become your words; your words become your actions; your actions become your habits; your habits become your lifestyle.* It then matters greatly what you think. If you do not like the direction your life is taking; change your thinking and speech.

There are people who are harvesting things that are discomforting and abrasive to their lives as a result of poor thinking, poor speaking, poor choices and wrong actions. On this note, the Bible says that a man reaps what he sows (Galatians 6:7). Always evaluate your own thinking, lest you inadvertently grow a field of weeds and nettles, rife with slugs and other nasties.

Make certain you remain true to yourself. Make certain that others do not get inside your head with negative philosophies or ideologies that corrupt you. Not everything that works for others will work the same for you. While you are similar to other humans in many ways, you are still very much different. Discover your uniqueness. Discover what works for you. Someone else's idea or plan might not be suitable to your life path.

Dreaming involves your mental faculties as well. You dream, you think, you plan, and you execute those plans. It all requires thoughtfulness and strategy. Without a wholesome, stable mind, this can prove difficult. A verse from the Bible tells us that a double-minded person is unstable in all their ways (James 1:8). When someone cannot make up their mind, and when they are indecisive and continually vacillate between decisions, they will remain unhinged and non-progressive. You cannot anchor your hopes on indecision. A ship has to be anchored in the harbour so it does not end up where the crew does not want it. Anchor yourself to a sure foundation so you are not tossed back and forth by the winds and storms of life.

If you lose your mind, you lose your way. If your thoughts are permanently glued to your past mistakes, offences, grudges or hurts, you might as well be playing "Stuck in the Mud" for all the progress you are making—or not making, rather. If you are not progressive in your thinking, change and transition can prove difficult. You must think ahead. Again, T. D. Jakes said, *"If your mind is always on where you have been, you will never get to where you're going."*

Your imagination is the place of creativity. Imagination is crucial. You get to dream up things in your mind long before they materialize outwardly. Some of the advances in technology or other fields you see unveiled today have been dreams in the hearts and minds of people who have carried those ideas or visions for years. I carried the dream or desire of being an author from the age of fourteen. That dream is now a reality, even after so many years. I also desired or dreamed of running my own business. That dream of being self-employed has since materialized, and I have written three books. This truly brings feelings of reward and satisfaction. This serves to positively fuel my other aspirations.

Many things affect the outworking and time frame of your dreams. Nevertheless, you must keep your mind focused until you accomplish your dreams. A strong mind helps you strongly execute your dreams; especially dreams that require years before they can become a reality. Remember, progress comes from the action you take regarding what you hear, say and believe. Passivity will keep you in a pool of stagnation.

Your mind or imagination is the place of incubation. Stay positive and motivated and speak life over your growing 'babies' (dreams and ideas). One needs a strong mind and heart to keep a dream alive. You limit your creativity and vitality if your mind is tired and overwhelmed. When you find yourself stressed out or tired mentally, take some time to recuperate. I love what William L Johnson II says: *"When your mind is tired, pull back and take a break. Find you a nice place with water or just soft music or silence. Give yourself time to regroup and refresh."*

Part of bringing a dream to bear is to be totally convinced in your mind that the dream is a possibility. Bear in mind that God never gives you dreams that cannot be fulfilled. Dreams, by nature, are an encouragement and reminder of future possibilities. Because dreams embody your purpose, you cannot afford to shelve or discard them, as I have pointed out earlier.

Decide to be a positive thinker, rather than a negative thinker. When you constantly feed yourself with a negative diet of pessimism, it is then hard to have a positive outlook. A renowned motivational speaker in his time, the late Hilary Hinton "Zig Ziglar" said, *"A negative thinker sees a difficulty in every opportunity. A positive thinker sees an opportunity in every difficulty."*

It is about finding hope and letting it dominate your thinking, which in turn helps you have a positive outlook. In the words of Lorri Faye: *"Being positive doesn't mean you don't ever have negative thoughts. It just means you don't let those thoughts control your life."*

If you think poorly of yourself or your aspirations, you will find it difficult to make your dreams a reality. You require confidence. You need to believe in your mind that you are valuable and unique, and have much to offer to the world. You must believe that your dreams matter. Your dreams have a place of significance in the timeline of history. Do not exit the planet without giving the best of yourself. Think of the kind of legacy you want to leave behind. Even if just one person benefits from your dream, it is worth it.

My friend, Pastor Emmanuel Might of Solid Rock Church in Dublin, Ireland, made a profound statement in one of his teachings regarding the mind: *"Defeat or victory begins within a man. If you can win the on-going battle in your mind, only then are you set to conquer your external and physical mountains. The greatest instrument for creating your success is not just money or your hands—it is mainly your mind. Your mind makes you rational, thoughtful, intellectual, imaginative and creative."*

If you do not think much of your dreams, no one else will. If you do not believe in your dreams, how can you expect others to? If you say you have no dreams, I say think again, because everyone has dreams. Take time to search your heart. Sometimes, a long lost and buried dream can resurface, and end up being the thing that catapults you to greatness and influence. Do your best not to leave your dreams dormant, especially those you are passionate about. By nurturing and protecting your dreams, you show that you treasure them.

Every human being encounters problems in life. Nevertheless, you do not need to spend great portions of your existence meditating on or wallowing in those problems. It is far better to think up solutions than just about the problems. Never be afraid of problems. Many times, problems are blessings in disguise, and can be a door to new opportunities, when correctly interpreted, and wisely handled. Some people's dreams emerge from problems. Therefore, do not just see a problem but also see an opportunity.

Many things you have acquired and experienced are answers to a problem. Water is an answer to thirst. Light is an answer to the problem of darkness. An aircraft, train, car or boat is an answer to a transport need. A stove or oven is an answer to the need for a cooked meal. Your dream could be a solution to a problem. Your dream could be an answer to a need. Your dreams are designed to benefit you and others. Being mindful of this will inspire you to fulfil your dreams in the face of seemingly insurmountable odds.

When the Israelites where in bondage and slavery in Egypt, God's dream was to use Moses to deliver them and take them to a far better place called the Promised Land (Exodus 3). There they would find peace, nourishment and vitality of life. When the world was enshrouded in sin and darkness, God's dream was a Saviour (John 3:16). Many times, the dream burning in your heart and mind is actually God putting his finger on a specific need he wants you to solve. God loves to collaborate with human beings in order to better their lives.

Many people are richer in their thinking than their bank accounts. Many people are richer in their thinking than where they live, what they wear or drive. This is not a bad thing. Money can run out and clothes and cars will get old, but your mind will not. Thinking is the one thing you cannot get away from or stop. You will still be thinking when you are old. Maybe not as sharply as before, but still, very much capable.

Most people want that great career, that great car, great house, great bank balance, or great relationship, and these are fine to have. However, a strong, great or rich mind is, by far, better. Would you rather have my money or my line of thinking? You are better off with my fruitful thinking. It is what helped get me the money. It does not cost money to think. Thinking is not a mistake or accidental occurrence. Be a purposeful thinker.

Sanity in any situation is a blessing; where you remain stable, balanced and unmoved by adverse circumstances or turbulences of life. This is garnered by realising that seasons and circumstances change. It is the attitude or forethought that there will be 'light at the end of the tunnel' that keeps you hopeful and perseverant. There is spring after winter; where once dead and withered things can be resuscitated and grow and blossom again. There is hope for that dream in your life that seams dead or in a winter season.

You are never defeated until you think and believe you are. People with a strong mind-set do not give up easily. They put up a fight. See your mind as a muscle that can be flexed. See your mind as a muscle that is able to be trained, developed and strengthened. Allow yourself to think big. Khanyah Arnez put it best when he said, *"Big things belong to people who think big."*

American industrialist Henry Ford did not give up on his dream of producing affordable automobiles. Rather, he thought big and eventually became the founder of the Ford Motor Company. He took his big dream to his own garage or workshop with a small team who believed in that dream. Those who initially rejected his dream probably wished they had not. Henry had a strong mind, not just a strong dream. That is why the world is full of amazing and affordable Ford cars. I have previously owned two different models. I was benefiting from Ford's dream.

Do not just limit your thinking to your initial ideas only. See how you can expand on them. Henry Ford did not just build vehicles for the road. Ford also entered the aviation business by building aircraft engines during World War I. His most successful aircraft was the Ford 4AT Trimotor (nicknamed the Tin Goose). It was the first successful US passenger airliner.

You must place before yourself a picture of victory. When your mind cannot picture what you desire or aim to accomplish, find a picture at which you can gaze. Mount it to your bedroom door or some place you will see it every day. This will help to keep you focused. One of the other ways is frequent meditation on your thoughts concerning your dreams. The things you think about frequently will dominate your mind. No person should want to think deeply and continually about negative or depressing things. If you ever desire a Scripture that encourages a positive thought life, then the Bible book of Philippians is the book for you:

> *"Finally, brethren, whatever things are true, whatever things are noble, whatever things are just [right], whatever things are pure [unpolluted], whatever things are lovely [beautiful and pleasing], whatever things are of good report [wholesome] . . . meditate on these things"* (Philippians 4:8, NKJV).

Arnold Schwarzenegger dreamed of becoming the world's greatest bodybuilder. One of the key things he did was place on his bedroom wall a photograph of Steve Reeves, a man who achieved the kind of success and career Arnold desired. Steve Reeves was a successful bodybuilder and actor. Schwarzenegger admirably said that Steve Reeves' amazing accomplishments gave him a sense of what was possible, even when others did not understand his dreams. It helped keep his dream alive. At the age of 20 he won the Mr Universe contest, and then went on to win Mr Olympia 7 times. What picture are you seeing? Where is your focus? Is it helping you see and stay focused on what you desire and wish to accomplish?

And note that Schwarzenegger was not confined to this one pathway for the duration of his life. He later came to see himself in film as an actor, and then channelled his thoughts and energy into acting. He gained worldwide fame as a Hollywood action film icon. If you think and believe you can accomplish great things, then you will. However, if you think and believe you cannot accomplish great things, then you probably will not. The output of your life is dependent on the input in your life, as far as your thoughts and actions are concerned. A chicken mentality will never elevate you to soar above the clouds like an eagle. Therefore, you must develop and possess an 'eagle mentality.'

Even after becoming a household name in Hollywood, Arnold's dreaming days seemed to have no end. Soon after the turn of the millennium, Schwarzenegger then saw himself playing a significant role in politics. He channelled those thoughts into reality, and became the governor of California. These massive achievements did not happen by chance. He had to put 'feet' to his thoughts. It all originated in his mind. He first saw it in his mind—the seat of great beginnings. Then it dropped down into his heart where it germinated. What are you seeing? What will germinate from what you envision and meditate on?

It matters greatly whose advice you accept. Be selective about who you allow to influence your thinking. You do not need depressing thoughts. You do not need negative thoughts that instil doubt, fear and discouragement. You do not need a pessimistic outlook on life. You do not need voices and thoughts that discourage your dreams, but rather those that encourage and lift you up.

The right company of people to keep are those who leave you feeling motivated and enthused about life, and about your dreams and goals. You need people who ooze with positivity. What is the point of hanging with people who deflate you?

Your thinking needs to be strong enough to deflect any negative input from others. Do not allow anyone to make you think less of yourself or your ideas. God does not think less of you, so why should you think less of yourself? Why allow others to make you think less of yourself?

There is a verse in the Bible book of Jeremiah where God informs mankind of how He views or thinks of them:

> *"For I know the thoughts that I think towards you, says the Lord, thoughts of peace and not evil, to give you a future and a hope"* (Jeremiah 29:11, NKJV).

This verse is amazing, for it shows that even God wants you to do well and succeed. God wants you to have a fruitful, peaceful and rewarding life.

How should you think? If you understand the different types of thinking, then you can use them to your advantage. You use your thinking skills to make decisions, solve problems, to organize things and to make sense of your experiences.

Types of Thinking:

1. Analytical (Convergent) Thinking: This allows you to gather all the facts and knowledge and piece things together. It allows you to see how you can best use what you gather to your advantage or that of others.

2. Creative Thinking: This kind of thinking is about coming up with new ideas or new ways of doing things. It is about taking what you know and putting things together in a fresh and imaginative way.

3. Divergent Thinking: The word diverge means *"to fan out or spread out."* This kind of thinking involves a person examining many things and then bringing them together to make decisions and solve problems. It is also about taking one great idea and expanding it.

4. Sequential Thinking: This thinking allows one to follow step-by-step processes so that their ideas progress logically. Sequential thinking enables one to follow certain steps that lead to the reality of their dreams.

5. Holistic Thinking: This type of thinking allows one to see the big picture. It is about the whole. All the facts, possibilities or factors are considered. You are able to ascertain how decisions and choices will affect the various areas of your life.

When bringing your dreams to pass, you use these various thinking types to make your dreams a reality. Your mind is a great tool. Use it to your benefit. Expand your thinking and your understanding regarding the birthing and execution of your dreams and ideas.

Heart Tug

It is good to do an inward inventory of yourself. Ask the hard questions:

- ➢ Who am I?
- ➢ Where am I heading?
- ➢ What do I want out of life? What plans am I making to achieve what I want?
- ➢ What desires, passions or dreams lie dormant in my heart?
- ➢ What am I willing to chase after with everything I have, no matter the cost?
- ➢ How much do I really want it?
- ➢ Will I make the sacrifices?
- ➢ What is tugging at my heart? What are my inclinations? What do I gravitate towards? What excites me? What brings me fulfilment?

You must be fearless in chasing after what sets your heart and soul on fire. When you are unsure of what to do, or the direction to take, follow your heart. Of course, it is wise to seek advice, but ultimately go with your heart. Be sensitive to that 'heart tug.'

As a boy of fourteen, Arnold Schwarzenegger said his parents had dreams or aspirations for his life. His father wanted him to become a police officer, while his mother wanted him to attend trade school. But he said, *"My own plan formed in my heart when I was fourteen years old."* That was the 'heart tug.' The dilemma was that it was not in any of the directions his parents wanted him to go. If he had forsaken his inward desire and dreams for what his parents wanted, we probably would never have heard of him. But he had a strong resolve concerning his dreams. His very own dreams took him from obscurity to being renowned and celebrated in an iconic manner. You should not negate your dreams in order to please the expectations others have or expect of you.

This kind of true, life story allows people to own their dreams and stand for their dreams in a resolute fashion. The things that bring joy, warmth and vigour to your heart are the things you should cherish and pursue. Your dreams will mean more to you than to others. Your task is to follow that tug in your heart. Do not let others lead you away from that.

People should not take over or reshape the things you purposed to achieve. Yes, take all the advice and assistance offered, but remain true to your original visions and dreams. Remain true and authentic to yourself. The lack of authenticity is because many want to be like someone else. You will be remembered better for just being you and not a version of some great original.

Your heart will not lie to you. Listen to it. Follow that inner voice. Many times, I get a sense or feeling about something that goes beyond my mental reasoning. The same can be true of your dreams. Your heart registers something about a dream that your mind plays catch up to. This might seem illogical, but let your mind follow your heart. However, just make sure you are not following deceptive or vain thoughts, imaginations or feelings that will only lead you into trouble or dead-ends.

The Bible book of Jeremiah 17:9 warns us that the heart is the most deceitful thing of all. Being led by good values and principles helps. It is bad enough for others to deceive you, but purely tragic to deceive yourself.

Choose to live by your chosen standards, and when you fail to meet them, re-align yourself with them. The best thing you can do for yourself when you fail is to try again. The other option is to stay defeated, which is the path of least resistance, but also one that will bury you and your dreams. Only dead things are buried. Your dreams have life. They do not die or end because you failed, but rather because you chose to give up.

God tends to guide people more from their hearts than their heads. When I do not have peace or calm about something, I tend to step cautiously, or stop completely. When I experience peace, calm and assurance about something, I proceed. I remember the heart tug I had when it came to settling for the right publisher regarding my very first book ("The Potential of Your Life"). Choosing my first publishing company was almost intuitive; almost instinctive. Each time I looked at a different publisher, I did not experience much peace and assurance in my heart. When I eventually settled on the initial publisher, that peace, calm and assurance returned. It was that sense of certainty that they were the right publisher for me; not that other publishers were not suitable. It is possible that I will write another book and sense that I need a different publisher. I am always conscious of that inner heart tug.

When you have several choices, what do you do? Listen to your heart. When all choices are good, try to find the one that will work the best for you. Another example was when I was getting ready to immigrate to Ireland. I was presented with three job offers in South Africa. It all came down to choice. I followed my heart and ended up in Ireland. What an amazing journey so far! I have accomplished so much, met so many great people, fulfilled some long overdue dreams and progressed further in many other areas (business, education, the arts and theology), and experienced many different places and cultures. Now I am a citizen of two countries.

When you are too cautious, and do not follow your heart, you could end up wishing you had. This is not how you want to look back over your life and feel. You do not want this regret. I was a very fast sprinter at school. In fact, when I left high school, no one was able to break my 100-metre record of 10:12 seconds. Many years after, I continued to win all the 100-metre parent races at the annual Sports Day. Who knows if I had pursued running seriously, I could have ended up like Usain Bolt, maybe—not as fast as him, but notably fast. Do I have some regrets about this? Yes, I do. Nevertheless, I am not dwelling on that, because there are other things I have pursued and been successful at.

Obviously, you cannot be the jack-of-all-trades and the master of none. Take one or two things and master them well. Then perhaps take on a third or fourth, if you find enough time, energy and passion. Herein you will find enrichment and see substantial progress. Trying to do too many things all at once will pull you in every direction, but not necessarily forward.

Be intentional. Have precise targets and aim to hit them with precision.

Doubt and uncertainty will always be there when you embark on fulfilling a great dream. There will be naysayers as well. Ignore them and listen to your heart. It is really a step of faith. Take all the encouragement from your supporters and press into your dreams. You were born to fulfil those dreams burning in your heart. The divine purpose for your life will never leave your life. It will always tug at your heart until you take notice and do something about it.

Determination

Determination is a crucial attribute you need. It helps undergird your willpower to persevere and endure. Without determination, quitting becomes easy and very tempting.

It is about deciding to follow through until the end or desired outcome of your dreams or goals. That decision to persevere ought to be settled at the start, not when the heat is on, or when your back is against the wall.

When you face huge challenges and adversity, I want you to remember the words of Henry Ford: *"When everything seems to be going against you, remember that the airplane takes off against the wind, not with it."*

An aeroplane has two powerful forces called *thrust* and *lift*. It does not matter what other forces operate against the plane, it will thrust ahead and soar into the sky. No matter what or who comes against you, God will always give you people and things that become like the force of *thrust* and *lift* to spear you ahead.

Previous failures or traumatic experiences should not stop you progressing. Rest, if you must. Take time to recover, if you must, but when you are done, get up and live your dreams. Be determined to make things happen irrespective of tragedy or set-backs. A founding father of psychoanalysis, the Swiss psychiatrist Carl Gustav Jung said, *"I am not what happened to me. I am what I choose to become."*

Determination is not just a cognitive state (of the mind or intellect), but also an affective state (involves emotions). It is that willpower and anticipatory enthusiasm, spurring you towards the finish, despite difficulties. Determination works best when you face adversity. You will know how determined you are by the adversity you face. So many people want a better life, but that will take determination and sacrifice.

When you are tempted to quit, just think of why you began in the first place. Think of that reward and satisfying feeling you will experience when your dream, idea or vision happens. No one gets accolades for starting things. Rather, rewards and accolades are given after your great achievements. The finish line is the beginning of reward.

I listened to an interview T.D. Jakes had with actor, producer and movie director Denzel Washington. Their conversation centred on Denzel's career. When you mention the name Denzel Washington, it commands attention, admiration and respect. He is a man who has achieved much and been rewarded and awarded greatly. But this recognition and those many accolades were not there when he was starting out, working hard and making those sacrifices. The glory only came afterwards. His hard work and sacrifices ushered him into the presence of some great people like Nelson Mandela, Bishop Desmond Tutu, T.D Jakes, Whitney Houston, Tom Hanks and Morgan Freeman.

If you only look for recognition and accolades, you could lose sight of real purpose and destiny. Accolades should not be the primary goal. They should rather be the fulfilment or satisfaction of accomplished purpose. The real and satisfying reward is knowing that you are fulfilling your purpose in life.

Denzel remained true to his purpose and destiny. In the interview, he mentioned that he is here to serve his family and the rest of humankind. That speaks of a man who is not intimidated or insecure by the success of others. He is a man who knows who he is and understands his God-given purpose on earth.

I was thrilled to be "Student of the Year" in my final school year, and thrilled when I received several awards at the awards banquet. As family, friends and teachers cheered and clapped for me, I thought back to the many hours of study. I thought of the late nights preparing. I thought of the provision my parents had given me throughout my schooling life that brought me to this pivotal point. It was suddenly all worth it. That moment of sweet joy and elation, knowing my hard work and sacrifice had paid off. Continue working hard and making those sacrifices. Pay Day is on the way!

Your dreams and goals will undergo many challenges, as will you, for they are your dreams. When you are sure of the potential and greatness of your dreams, do not quit. On the other hand, quitting is not a bad thing if you are giving up something that is harmful or unbeneficial to you.

Many people determine to quit things that are negative to their well-being. Determination will help you to quit and stay out, if that is what you need. Likewise, determination will help you not to quit, if that is what is required concerning your situation.

The struggles of life come to everyone. No one is exempt. Everyone has to deal with the pressures of life and other challenges, whether in health, relationships, careers or finance. You are not alone. That is why you can lean on others who have endured, and who have overcome a struggle you may be presently experiencing. It is comforting to have someone in your corner when you are fighting great battles. Those who gather around a fighter or boxer in the corner of the ring, are there to attend to him or her, but also to encourage them to fight on and to see the match through to the end. Simply put, that team is keeping the fighter determined. Who are the people in your corner to keep you determined?

When I train at my local gym, I struggle against those weights. There is sweat and effort and pain or muscle stress, but the reward is that I become stronger and fitter. I usually look forward to my training sessions. It is a bonus to look forward to something, which will benefit you, even when you know it will require great effort and dedication. Because I am determined, I keep going. I refuse to procrastinate. I may take a few breaks, or moments to rest, but I am not retiring. I am the kind of person who is determined to work beyond the conventional retirement age.

As long as you have breath in your body, you do not have to stay down or defeated. Failure and setbacks should not be your end. Dust yourself off and take another shot at it. If it did not work out the first time, try again. Many times, it is in the 'trying again' when breakthrough comes. What do you do if you fail the second and third time? You try again. Scientist and inventor Thomas Edison made a thousand unsuccessful attempts before getting the light bulb to work. A friend of mine failed her driving test four times. I am not going to tell you her name. Anyone would be frustrated with themselves and the driving inspector after so many fails. Determined to get that license, she decided to try again for the fifth time—and she passed. She was thrilled to receive her licence. Did it have to take this long? No, but at least she stayed the course until victory was secured. Her four fails did not cancel out her chance of passing or winning because she decided to press on past failure. She refused to quit. Treat failure as a bump in the road, not the end of the road.

Determination does not take into account how many times one has to get up and try again. It is about that tenacity in you that refuses to quit no matter how many valleys you have to endure. Anyone can feel strong and unrelenting against challenges when they are standing in victory on the mountaintop, but can they still feel strong and unrelenting in the face of failure or discouragement in the valley? That is where true strength, or the lack of it thereof, is exposed.

Filmmaker and funny man Tyler Perry has a unique story of chasing one's dreams, no matter what obstacles are in the way. Most times when we produce something, we think it is going to be an immediate hit or great success. Indeed, this does happen in certain cases, yet it did not for Tyler's first scripted stage play. In fact, it was a financial failure, receiving a "less than stellar" reception. Tyler Perry had invested $12,000 of his own money, which in the 90's was a substantial amount of money. Nevertheless, he did not give up. Determination helped him stay the course. He was quite discouraged, yet still determined.

Failure should not automatically lead to quitting. You can start over. New York Times bestselling author and charismatic speaker Joyce Meyer said, *"You can begin again. Whoever you are, wherever you are, whatever you've been through, it's never too late to begin again."*

In the face of failure and setback, Tyler Perry did not hang up his gloves. He continued to write, improve his skill, and do more shows. He eventually gained more followers and approval. His work was recognized. His financial earnings spiked. In due course, he became a millionaire. The messages of hope, forgiveness, challenges and restoration in his movies resonated with millions of people. He remained true to his dreams, and they eventually paid off. Your dreams are designed to make your life better. It may take a while, but it will eventually happen for you.

Tyler Perry did not have an easy upbringing, but was able to use all the pain, shame and frustrations to fuel his dreams. In fact, his dream of becoming a writer stemmed from trying to work out his problems through the medium of writing. That career in writing opened up other areas for him over time. He became an author, producer, actor and director of his own movies that are quite popular. He also became the proud founder and owner of Tyler Perry Studios in Atlanta Georgia.

You must devote yourself wholly to your dream or idea. Be determined to make it happen. Fear and uncertainty will show up. Be determined to overcome them. When you have determination up front, then fear and uncertainty must take a backseat. You will need that element of faith, as you step into places and things you have not previously experienced. Faith will help to stabilize and reinforce your trust and belief in your dreams and their outworking. Never forget that God is on your side, and He wants you to have *milestones* and *breakthroughs*.

Long-range dreams will require more determination and patience. Learn to enjoy the process or journey that leads you to the fruition of your dreams. It is easier to endure the process of a short-term goal than a long-term one. Long-range goals will need to be insulated against fatigue, quitting or dissipating passion.

Success needs determination. Olympic gold medallist James Cleveland "J.C./Jesse" Owens said, *"We all have dreams. But in order to make dreams come to reality, it takes an awful lot of determination, dedication, self-discipline, and effort."*

If you want to be successful, you need to be determined, because true and lasting success hardly happens overnight. I am more impressed by those who are determined to succeed than those who are destined to succeed. There will be days when you wake up and are excited about your dreams and goals. Equally, there will be days when you do not feel or see your dreams as exciting and worth pursuing. There will be days when you are clueless as to how you will bring your dreams to pass. This is when you have to do what needs to be done to advance your dreams and goals, irrespective of how you feel. Remember, you are the one responsible for creating the kind of life you want to wake up to. Instead of falling into self-pity and blaming the adverse circumstances, rather, press through those circumstances. Always tell yourself that there is light at the end of the tunnel.

Be a REBEL in the pursuit of your dreams. Rebel against doubt, against fear and naysayers. Rebel against quitting; against apathy and self-pity. If there was ever a suitable time to be a rebel, it is when faced with such negative things that block your progress as a dreamer. You were born to dream and win, not quit and lose. Have hope that you will be successful, even at the inception of your dreams. See the acorn tree in the acorn seed.

Protecting Your Dreams

Be ready to protect your dreams, just as parents would protect their children. Own your dreams, and stand by your dreams. When you have things of great value in your home, you usually keep them in a safe place or location, like a safe. Not just anyone can access those treasures. Only those you trust can. You ought to protect your dreams, ideas and vision in much the same way. If someone or something is dear to your heart, you will make certain that person or thing is well protected and nurtured.

There are plenty of situations and people to discourage you in some way. You must remain tenacious against such attacks on your dreams. People who do not value your dreams are unlikely to support and encourage you. People who are jealous of you will not want to see you fulfil your awesome God-given dreams. People ought to be inspired by your greatness, not jealous or intimidated by it.

Do not let people slay or sabotage your dreams. Be wise and selective with whom you share your dreams and desires. You have to guard your dreams and ideas that are still in their infantile stages. People will seek to steal your dreams and ideas at a 'drop of a hat' and pass them off as their own. Others will determine to cause you to abandon or abort your dreams and ideas through belittlement. Find people who will speak life over your dreams. You do not need to succumb to people who speak death over your dreams and ideas. You must continue to speak positively over yourself and your dreams.

When people cannot aim high themselves, they try to discourage those who do. Former First Lady of the United States of America, Michelle Obama related a story of how she dreamed of going to the best university. She had high expectations. Many people told her she was setting her sights too high. They reasoned that a girl like her could not get into an elite institution. Those who discouraged her high expectation were trying to put her into their own narrow and limited box. After a while, she started to wonder if they were right. However, she proved them wrong and met her initial expectations for greatness. She attained a law degree, became an NGO director, and a hospital executive; and all this before she became the first lady and a world-famous icon.

Obviously, you will share your ideas with others to get their view or advice. However, try to remain committed to what is in your heart concerning your dreams. Revert to your passion and belief in those dreams and ideas. Find things and people who will feed your passion and belief concerning your dreams. Find the correct *recipes* that fan your dreams into flame. If you want to go up, find things and people who will help you go up. Motivational speaker, Dr Dave Martin said, *"People are like elevators. Some take you down or take you up. Get around those who take you up."*

Some people will be threatened or intimidated by your dreams and ideas. Do not let them stop you. King Saul antagonized his son-in-law and up-and-coming King David. Saul's negative reactions towards David stemmed from his jealousy of David. Saul felt threatened, in fact, that he even tried to kill David. This historical account is recorded in the Bible in the book of Samuel and Chronicles. You do not need to entertain people in your life who feel better when you fail or struggle. You are not a doormat or footstool to be trampled on.

Not everyone feels great about your successes. In the Bible, young Joseph had two great dreams. He was intrigued and passionate about them, whereas his brothers were completely jealous and annoyed just at the mention of those dreams. Genesis 37:18-19 reads:

> *"Now when they saw him afar off, even before he came near them, they conspired against him to kill him. Then*

they said to one another, 'Look, this dreamer is coming.
Come therefore, let us kill him and cast him into some pit;
and we shall say, 'Some wild beast has devoured him. We
shall see what will become of his dreams!'" (NKJV).

Joseph's brothers attempted to destroy his dreams by destroying him. Some people love you until you present a great dream or until you are promoted. Then, at the turn of a dime, they go from loving you to hating you, as your great dream or higher position triggers the exposure of anxieties and detestations they had hidden in their hearts. Joseph's brother's attempt to kill him did not materialize: Joseph's older brother, Reuben, spoke up for him and found a way to circumvent his death, and the result was that Joseph was instead sold into slavery. His brothers took him away from his dear father and away from family to a foreign land. Nevertheless, he was alive, and that meant he had a fighting chance at seeing his dreams come to pass. He was on a difficult road and in a difficult place that seemed to be carrying him away from his dreams. However, God was able to use the adverse circumstances to push him towards his destiny.

Protecting your dreams is also much like a farmer would protect his crop by eradicating the weeds and pests that are harmful. One of the main reasons people lock up their cars and houses is to keep the thief out. They are keeping out what is potentially harmful to their treasure. If you treasure your dreams, you will keep the dream slayers and pessimistic people away from influencing those dreams negatively.

Everyone seems to have an opinion, especially when it concerns you. Not everyone is qualified or entitled to speak into your life. Not everyone's advice is beneficial or suitable to your situation. You are not obliged to take everyone's advice. Be selective. Choose your advisers wisely. There is a story of a king who took the foolish advice of some of his peers who were serving him. This king by the name of Rehoboam, rejected the sound advice of the older wise men. The result was that he ended up losing his position as king (2 Chronicles 10).

Do not be the destroyer of your own dreams by beating yourself down and belittling your dreams. You have to be ready to defend your dreams no matter what. Become the advocate or solicitor of your own dreams. Fight for their acquittal into the limelight of destiny; instead of condemning them to the chains of darkness and extinction. Your dreams must live.

If you study literature, you will learn about the different kinds of conflicts in which human beings can find themselves. Even moviemakers and writers use one, two, or all of these three kinds of conflicts in their stories.

> ➤ Man against man
> ➤ Man against nature
> ➤ Man against himself

At one point or another, we must all deal with outer and inner conflict. Many times, internal battles end up crippling people's potential and momentum, if not dealt with. People tend to be better at dealing with the enemy on the outside than the one inside. Do not become the enemy of your own dreams. Do not become the enemy of your own destiny. I think it is quite tragic to sabotage your own destiny.

In the emotionally-charged movie titled The Pursuit of Happyness, there is a scene where Will Smith tells his son: "DON'T EVER LET SOMEONE TELL YOU THAT YOU CAN'T DO SOMETHING, NOT EVEN ME. YOU GOT A DREAM, YOU GOT TO PROTECT IT. PEOPLE CAN'T DO SOMETHING THEMSELVES, THEY WANT TO TELL YOU, YOU CAN'T DO IT. YOU WANT SOMETHING, GO AND GET IT. PERIOD."

I could not have said it any better. In the pursuit of your dreams, the above quote is paramount. Read it again and never forget it. Do not let anyone tell you that you cannot do something you are passionate about doing. Either you passionately pursue your dreams, or you can let others subject you to a mediocre life. Eagles do not hang around chickens. Eagles live and function on a higher level. Be like an eagle. Live and function on a higher level; and do not apologize for it.

It is important who you listen to and who you follow. Nobody wants the advice of someone who only sees and speaks gloom and doom. People have enough troubles and challenges of their own. Therefore, it makes sense that they would gravitate towards those people who encourage and uplift them. That is why many people gravitated towards Jesus. He offered hope, love, peace, joy, healing, forgiveness and abundant life. This is evident throughout the Gospels of Matthew, Mark, Luke and John. If you are going to fly a kite, you will need wind. Find those people who will be like the wind to cause your dreams to fly high. Gravitate toward dream builders, not dream slayers.

It is understandable that people get to profit from your dreams, especially those who help you. However, you do not need people who are only interested in what they can gain, but have no interest in your well-being and life. If what someone gains from you causes you to suffer loss or brings you stress or discomfort, then you need to re-evaluate that relationship. It should be a mutual relationship, not a parasitic one. True supporters do not just benefit from you, but help you benefit from them. True supporters have your best interest at heart, not just their own.

People who stay loyal to you only as long as they are getting something from you are not loyal or genuine friends. Some people are like leaches or parasites. They want to benefit from your dreams, but add nothing to help. They are too lazy or apathetic to work on their dreams and goals. As long as someone else is meeting their immediate needs, they are quite happy to remain unproductive in life. People in your life will either nourish you or deplete you. Choose wisely those you want close to you. Make sure each person close to you is someone who nourishes, not one who depletes or drains you.

Jesus demonstrated true friendship and support toward humankind by giving up His life for all. A record of this is found in John, chapter 15:13. It says:

> *"Greater love has no one than this, than to lay down his life for his friends"* (NKJV).

Laying down one's life for someone is not just about sacrificing one's own life to save them, but also about using one's time, resources, and energy to help others. It is about being there for others when they need you most. Many people have lost their lives trying to save others, whether rescuing them from a burning building or from drowning, or some other life-threatening situation. These are noble acts of heroism. Jesus gave up His life and suffered a cruel death on the cross for humankind. This was one of our greatest needs: a need for a Saviour. We can count Jesus as a true and loyal friend.

The Value of Your Dreams

Value simply means *"something that is dear, important, worthwhile and very useful.* When something is valuable, it is *good, beneficial, helpful and profitable."* Your daily life is lived out of your *principles, standards, convictions and beliefs*. You can tell where someone's life is heading just by these four aspects.

Values define who you are. They create necessary boundaries to govern your life. Values anchor you and hold things together in your life. They create a centre point around which you revolve or live. They allow for a consistency around the things you hold dear. If you value something, you will protect it. How you treat a thing indicates how much you value it. For example, if you value your happiness, then you will not allow people to take it from you. You will not do things that threaten that happiness. If you value unity, then you will do all you can to keep unity. Parents protect, love and discipline their children because they value them. When you value your dreams, you will protect, nurture and love them, and be passionate about them.

When you buy a house, usually the agent will send someone out to evaluate the house or property. They sum up its value and worth. Through the evaluation, you are then able to determine whether it is worthwhile buying or investing in that property. No one wants to waste resources on something that is of little or no value. The same would apply if you were buying a vehicle or buying stocks or shares in some company. You want to make sure you will get a good return for your investment. No one invests resources to lose them. You want to gain. You want a harvest.

Approaching your dreams with this attitude is important. If you value your dreams, you will go to great lengths to invest in them. I cannot foresee people investing in something they are not serious about, or to which they are not committed. One instance of this in the Bible is when twin brother Esau neglected his birthright and the blessing tied to it. For those who are unfamiliar with the narrative, Esau one day came in from hunting, parched and hungry. His brother, Jacob, had cooked some food. Naturally, Esau requested some of this food from his brother. Jacob, being a trickster, decided to trade his tasty food for his brother's birthright. Esau's response to this indicated that he did not value his birthright. Genesis 25:29-33 says:

> *"Now Jacob cooked a stew; and Esau came in from the field, and he was weary. And Esau said to Jacob, 'Please feed me with that same red stew, for I am weary [tired and hungry].' But Jacob said, 'Sell me your birthright as of this day.' And Esau said, 'Look, I am about to die [from hunger]; so what is this birthright to me?' Then Jacob said,*

> *'Swear by me as of this day.' So he swore to him, and sold*
> *his birthright to Jacob. And Jacob gave Esau bread and*
> *stew of lentils; then he ate and drank, arose, and went*
> *his way. Thus Esau despised his birthright"* (NKJV).

Treating it as unworthy or useless, Esau consequently scorned his birthright. This later came back to haunt him. He lost the rights and privileges of the first-born, and the great blessing that came with it. To say it another way, Esau sold his precious and valuable birthright for something far less valuable in order to satisfy a carnal, temporary urge. Sometimes people sell their dreams for a moment of pleasure or emotional hype. Esau obviously did not think things through. He threw away his blessing and privilege. He did regret it later on.

Do not let someone else value your dreams more than you do. You will be sorry and bitter when they are successful with your dreams because you despised them. Hold the things you value close to your heart. Hold your dreams close to you. They are dear or valuable to you. They are your future. They are the outworking of your destiny. The apostle Paul was passionate about completing the ministry God gave him. He said:

> *". . . but one thing I do, forgetting those things which are*
> *behind and reaching forward to those things which are*
> *ahead, I press toward the goal for the prize of the upward*
> *call of God in Christ Jesus"* (Philippians 3:13-14) NKJV.

When a man or woman values their partner and children, they will make great sacrifices to meet the needs of their family. They offer love, support and protection for their family. The same applies to the friends we have. We will love and treat them with respect because we value them. In fact, every human being ought to be valued and respected.

Passion for Your Dreams

Passion is what drives your dreams. It is like a force that ignites desire inside you to go after what you want. It is what sets your soul on 'fire.' Passion is a *"strong emotion towards something. It is a strong feeling of excitement that causes you to act in a certain way."*

Passion affects many areas of your life. It affects your emotions, your sexual drive and other appetites, your relationships, your career, your dreams, your hopes, and your ambitions. A person is capable of doing many things passionately. They can love or hate passionately. They can be passionate about health, the environment or human rights. They can be passionately nurturing or caring.

Obviously, it is better to be passionate about positive things. Prolonged anger or hate can lead to destructive actions or behaviour. Your passions affect you and the people around you. Do your best to affect them positively. It helps to control your impulse to lash out at others. Take some time to cool down. Re-evaluate and decide on a constructive response to a negative situation. This is not always easy but possible. Passion negatively channelled, if left unchecked, can cause you to sabotage your dreams and relationships.

Passion allows you to put more energy and work into what you want to achieve. It provides the excitement and enthusiasm that helps to drive your dreams forward. Passion keeps you excited, not just at the inception of your dream, but during the process that leads to its achievement. Passion will help keep your dreams alive, long after the start. Passion makes the process and duration of a dream endurable and exciting. Bob Kennedy said, *"When you attach passion to your dream, you get yourself closer to achieving it."*

I was passionate about writing this book. It was a long process of study, research, prayer and organizing of ideas and information. Then came the editorial work on the content, layout, cover design and blurb. The marketing aspects and other factors come after this. Eventually there comes the unhidden joy bubbling to the surface, when I get to see the book in print and in the hands of many readers.

Passion and desire are linked together. Desire is a *"strong want for something. It is a strong craving, longing or yearning for something."* Passion is the conduit and force that allows and drives you to pursue what you want. Without passion, desire can remain dormant.

Just like dreams, your passion will reveal your purpose. If you cannot discover your purpose, then check what you are passionate about. Some people are passionate about writing, so they become writers. Some people are passionate about racing, so they pursue racing. Others may be passionate about acting, so they become actors. It is quite easy to figure out what people are passionate about. All you need to do is observe what they love doing and where their focus lies.

Passionate people make things happen. They refuse to coast along in life. They do not sit on the fence. Mediocrity does not impress them. Obstacles do not discourage them. Bar Rafaeli, a renowned model from Israel, said, *"Have the passion, take the action and magic will happen."*

The passion you have for something leads to the magnification and greatness of that thing. It is like magic. It will put joy in your heart, a sparkle in your eye and a smile on your face. That is how I felt when my first published hardcopy book arrived in the post. This is how I felt many years ago when I became a fully qualified teacher. This is how I felt when I recently landed a role in a few movies.

You will encounter trials and failure, but do not lose your passion. Mythologist and writer Joseph Campbell said, *"Passion will move men beyond themselves, beyond their shortcomings, beyond their failures."* Many times, people have overcome their fear and inadequacy by the shear passion, desire and determination for something. Go after all you want with all your heart. Half-hearted efforts hardly produce anything great. Mediocrity is the result of feigned passion.

How do you keep your passion alive? Focus on what you love. Focus on your dreams. It is difficult to discourage a highly passionate person. You do not mind sacrificing for something for which you are passionate. Jesus paid a high cost. He paid with His life to redeem people. It was a great sacrifice to die such a cruel death on the cross; nevertheless, He did it because He was passionate about redeeming people and changing their lives for the better.

The Champion in You

Muhammad Ali said, *"To be a great champion you must believe you are the best. If you're not, pretend you are."*

By definition, a CHAMPION is a *"person who has defeated or conquered all opponents and claimed first position or first prize."* Being a champion speaks of being a victor. It speaks of being an overcomer. A champion is somebody who was once a contender who refused to quit. To him or her, winning is not an option but a MUST.

You must become the champion of your dreams. Do not quit until you win. Muhammad Ali also said, *"Champions are made from something they have deep inside of them—A desire, a dream, and a vision."* Arnold Schwarzenegger echoed this when he said, *"Champions are not born, they are built."*

Determination, desire, passion and hard work are the building blocks of championship. Being a champion starts in your heart. Find it there. Nurture it and grow it. You cannot afford to be average when it comes to your dreams. Be willing to push things to the edge, and to the limit. Go all the way. Do it right, or do not attempt it at all. As I have said previously, half-baked efforts never fully rise to anything great.

Athlete Leon Brown said, *"Never underestimate your own strength. You were born for a purpose and are blessed with the power to achieve it."* Champions believe their dreams are significant, and that they will make a difference. Making a difference can be scary, but it is necessary. Martin Luther King Jr. had a dream to see equal civil rights for African Americans.

It was a good dream and a necessary dream. Martin Luther King paid the ultimate price for his dream. Today many still benefit from his dream. He is remembered mostly for his "I HAVE A DREAM" speech. This historic speech, delivered on the steps of the Lincoln Memorial, helped to galvanize the Civil Rights Movement. This speech resonated with the national and international audience. Here are a few lines from King's speech.

"I have a dream that one day this nation will rise up and live out the true meaning of its creed. We hold these truths to be self-evident: that all men are created equal."

"I have a dream that my four children will one day live in a nation where they will not be judged by the colour of their skin but by the content of their character."

"Now is the time to lift our nation from the quicksand of racial injustice to the solid rock of brotherhood."

"Let us not seek to satisfy our thirst for freedom by drinking from the cup of bitterness and hatred."

If you stumble and fall, GET BACK UP! GET BACK ON TRACK AND MOVE CLOSER TO YOUR DREAMS AND GOALS. THIS YOU CAN DO! Champions look for possibilities, not excuses. You must endeavour to think like a champion, train like a champion and fight for your dreams like a champion. Champions are too busy getting better, so they have no time for excuses. They have no time to succumb to naysayers, fear and average living.

Many champions will tell you that they have failed at times. They have experienced setbacks and great challenges. Then they will also tell you that giving up is not in their vocabulary. Your dreams are too important for you to give up on them at the first sign of difficulty. People who make too many excuses are not fired up to fight and win. They have not placed a high value on their dreams. They are willing to settle for a mediocre life. You are God's V.I.P on earth, so live above mediocrity.

For me, a true and great champion is one who not only fights for himself, but for the people. Martin Luther King Jr. fought for the people; for civil rights in a non-violent way. Nelson Mandela fought for the people; for civil rights and equality. Mahatma Gandhi fought for the independence from a British-ruled India. There are many others. Their hearts were too big for selfish ambitions. They were too passionate and generous to live only for themselves.

Jesus stands as a great champion of the souls of men and women. He got in the ring and boxed the Devil's 'lights' out, so to speak. Jesus endured the ridicule, the false accusations and the beatings. He took the crown of thorns and the nails on the cross, as well as the spear that pierced his side. He endured the shame and cruelty of the cross. He died to save people from damnation. Then He rose again to life. There is perhaps no greater victor and champion in history. The account of Jesus' life is found mainly in the four Gospels of Matthew, Mark, Luke and John.

You are better off working hard for what you want, than wishing hard for what you want. If you want something, you must go after it. You must be willing to pay the price. When a man truly falls in love with a woman, he goes after her with all his heart, attempting to convince her of his love. You must go after what you want with all your heart. Half-hearted efforts show a lack of commitment, passion and excellence. In the Bible, 1 Corinthians 9:24 says:

> *"Do you not know that those who run in a race all run, but one receives the prize. Run in such a way that you may obtain it. And everyone who competes for the prize is temperate [self-disciplined] in all things"* (NKJV).

In other words, do your best to win. Live a disciplined, self-controlled life to help you gain that prize. Living an undisciplined life can hamper your progress and achievement of great things.

Champions do not need to be bribed or coerced into achieving great things. They are willing to walk away from things that lack integrity or authenticity. They do not want to buy their way to greatness, but work their way there. They are prepared to remain true to themselves even if it means it will take longer to accomplish their dream.

Champions are willing to learn, to grow, and to be empowered. They find people who will inject life into them, and who will stir them deeply and awaken them to higher levels. They do not underestimate the power of others to fuel their passion and drive them forward.

The day you become a champion is most likely not the day the world discovers it. When David (as a teenager) slew the lion and the bear in order to protect the sheep, no one witnessed it. It all happened in private. David was having great success privately. He had become a champion privately. No one was there to see it, celebrate it and cheer David on. However, David did not deliver the sheep from the lion and bear to get the applause of people. Rather, he did it because he loved the sheep, and was responsible for them. He did it because he was made of champion material.

When David faced Goliath, the Philistine, in a public setting, I am sure many of the Israelites thought he was foolish and naïve. They probably thought that Goliath would kill him. After all, Goliath was a giant, experienced in war and fighting. However, David had a unique experience of his own with dealing with enemies—plus David had a secret weapon; his faith and confidence in God to give him victory (1 Samuel 17:33-35). God was on His side. Have you ever won a battle or achieved something great where you knew it could not have just been your own ability? You had divine help.

By the time it was all over, Goliath was dead and David was the victor. He was a champion who had stepped onto the public stage. He won in private, and now he was winning in public. Do not despise your hidden or private successes. Soon or later, they will benefit you in the public arena. The private arena is your training ground. The public arena is the showground and place of challenge where you secure victory followed by celebration.

A tall oak or cedar tree looks majestic and strong. You see this part. What you cannot see are its roots that go way down deep into the ground. Their purpose is to anchor the tree, provide stability and draw minerals for the tree. Without these strong roots, there would be no majestic and strong tree above ground. Champions know that they have to root themselves deeply to withstand any test or trial in the public setting.

I believe there are many people carrying great dreams the world has not seen or heard of yet. They are in preparation. They are working hard. They are making huge sacrifices. Most people only get to see a champion in his or her glorious moment, but they do not see all the hard work, sweat and tears that brought them to that glorious moment. When no one else is looking, the champion is hard at work; making great sacrifices. His or her 'roots' are growing down deep to support a tall dream.

All champions have high expectations. They have clear goals. They aim high. They adopt a certain lifestyle to reach the pinnacles of success in whatever arena they are. True champions accept the challenges. Many times champions have to motivate themselves. They cannot always rely on others for motivation.

Champions use challenges, adverse circumstances and setbacks to rise to greatness. They work on turning the impossible to what is possible. What are you doing with your troubles and difficulties? Constant complaining about them does not make you champion material. Overcoming them is what makes you champion material.

Champions set 'big targets' for there is more to 'aim' at. They are more interested with hitting the target than allowing the target to intimidate them. If placed in a giant stadium or room, will you feel small and intimidated? Do not let the hugeness of the challenge make you feel small or insignificant. The hugeness of your surroundings or challenge does not have to diminish your inner strength and greatness. See with the eyes of greatness. A champion spirit is larger than life. It is larger than the circumstance.

When the Chicago Cubs won their first baseball title in 108 years, it was an electric moment for them. They rallied from 3-1 deficit to win the MBL World Series against the Cleveland Indians in 2016. It was explosive for the team and fans. The joy was totally unrestrained. I am certain every fan was more than proud to wear the Cubs T-shirt. The Cub team were champions in the eyes of their fans. They had tasted the sweetest success as a team. In January 2017, they were guests at the White House, where they were saluted and celebrated. Each of those team members will tell you that it took hard work, determination and tenacity to win and enjoy sweet celebration.

No amount of challenge should quell (subdue or suppress) your desire and passion to be a champion. The success that is within you will eventually manifest outwardly. The world may not see it just yet, but you know you have it. Champions do not run from challenges, but they overcome them. Champions decide within themselves that they are pressing forward, not cowering back.

Most people probably have watched all the Rocky movies. They probably have been inspired by the Rocky Balboa character that Sylvester Stallone played. He champions the course of the underdog in all the Rocky films in the Rocky franchise. The basic theme is about Rocky Balboa overcoming a worthy opponent. We see in the final fight of his life, Rocky coming out of retirement, donning his gloves again and going up against the current, reigning, heavyweight champion. He overcomes all the obstacles, claims the victory, and reveals to everyone that he is still the real champ.

Maybe giant challenges face you. Nevertheless, you want to win; you want to achieve. You want to go after those dreams you placed on retirement. You want a glorious future. Just as Rocky Balboa did, go ahead and fight. Release that champion in you.

I personally have a few champions who inspire me greatly. These are real life champions. They are my personal heroes:

> Elizabeth Margret Morris (my mother, homemaker and a very fine cook). She gave birth to me in 1974. She sent me to school, including my twelve siblings. She could not read or write, but she managed our home well, and even learnt to drive. She worked very hard, and always put her children first. She taught us to work hard. She taught us to be honest and upright. She trained us to be clean, respectable and polite. She loved us unconditionally. She was caring and sensitive. She was the best female champion in my life.

> Arnold Schwarzenegger (actor, bodybuilder, philanthropist and politician). Here is a man who was willing to follow his dreams no matter what. He had faith and hope, and rose from obscurity to stardom. He encouraged and inspired many people. He did not just positively reshape his own life, but that of others as well. He helped turn body building into a worldwide, celebrated sport. His health and fitness programmes positively affected many youth and adults. He is a real life hero and champion.

➤ Denzel Washington (actor, filmmaker, director and producer). A failing student, who took the opportunities presented and carved a pathway for himself in the film industry to become a household name. He is a father, husband and true gentleman. He is a man who unashamedly expresses his belief and reliance on God, and his love and service to family and fellowman.

➤ Bishop T.D Jakes (pastor, author and filmmaker, philanthropist and businessperson). Perhaps for me, Jakes is one of the greatest preachers and inspirations as far as spirituality and other practical life issues are concerned. He is a man who started out from humble beginnings. Through the early years of his ministry, he started out with ten members in his church. Today he pastors a church with about 30,000 members. He is very gifted at speaking into the lives of people who are broken or hurting. He is a prolific communicator who communicates directly to the heart of man. He remains passionate about God and about helping people.

➤ Wayne Thring (pastor, politician, teacher and deputy president of the A.C.D.P.). Wayne rose against the challenges of an alcoholic father and racial injustices in South Africa to become a pastor, politician, father and husband. He is a true role model for many. He mixes faith and politics, speaking for those less fortunate, as well as boldly declaring that leaders and governments need God, and should govern with integrity. He just so happens to be the one who mentored me over the former years of my life. He invested time, wisdom and resources in my life and that of my family. It was an honour to have him endorse my first book (*The Potential of Your Life*, as well as my third book titled *Why Is God So Good?*).

> The late Nelson Mandela (lawyer, politician, civil rights activist, former president of South Africa and philanthropist). I will always be proud of Nelson Mandela. He is a true hero, who fought for equality and justice for those oppressed by the then apartheid government of South Africa. He was truly a father of the nation.

I could name a few more of my personal heroes. I am sure you could too. Ask yourself why you chose those particular people as your champions or heroes. How do they inspire you? What lessons did they teach you, and how are you applying them to your life?

Dealing with Fear

Fear is a very real factor that has to be addressed. It must be understood and then dealt with. By definition, fear is the *"unpleasant emotion caused by the belief that something or someone is dangerous, or is likely to cause you harm or pain."*

To say you have never experienced fear would be a lie. Everyone fears something, and has to deal with or overcome that fear. People can fear a myriad of things. One can fear the future, or the unknown; one can fear heights or small spaces; one can fear sickness or death; one can fear ridicule or criticism; one can fear losing a job; one can fear an exam or addressing a crowd; the list is somewhat endless.

You have to make a choice to face your fears, not run from them. There is a saying: **FEAR EVERYTHING AND RUN OR FACE EVERYTHING AND RISE.** You cannot afford to let fear and intimidation hinder your dreams. You cannot stress or worry too much about what others will say or think about you or your dreams. There are things you know are good to do, but you shrink back for fear of the reactions or opinions of others. Rosa Parks said, *"You must never be fearful about what you are doing when it is right."*

Even God does not want you to fear. In fact, the Bible mentions the phrase: "DO NOT FEAR" 365 times. That is one for every day of the year. Fear does not originate with God. The Bible tells us that God has not given us a spirit of fear, but of love, power and a sound (strong and stable) mind (2 Timothy 1:7). God tells people not to fear, for He promises to be with them. Isaiah 41:10 says:

"Fear not, for I am with you; Be not dismayed, for I am your God. I will strengthen you. Yes, I will help you. I will uphold you with My right hand" (NKJV).

God does not want you to be fearful or insecure about your future, your abilities or dreams. T.D. Jakes said, *"Fear can make you give up something that God wants to use to bless you."* Do not fear what God is doing in your life. Do not fear the way He has gifted you. Celebrate your uniqueness, instead of shelving it. Do not be afraid to display who you are. Uniqueness is a blessing. The world can be a far better place when we celebrate our differences, instead of fighting over them. Different is good. Variety is good. It would be boring if we were all the same, and did everything the same.

A certain level of confidence is required. If you really think about it, people are actually stronger and braver than they realize. Tap into your strength and courage, then watch your fears and insecurities diminish. Remember, your Creator does not come to make you weak, but rather to make you strong. He told Joshua to be two things: one, STRONG and two, COURAGEOUS. God repeated these encouraging words to Joshua three times in chapter one of the Bible book of Joshua. Let me quote one of them from Joshua 1:9:

"Have I not commanded you? Be strong and of good courage; do not be afraid, nor be dismayed, for the LORD your God is with you wherever you go" (NKJV).

There are two aspects of fear. There is a *negative fear* that is unhealthy. This fear is what hinders people from being all they purpose to be. This fear has a crippling effect. This fear is intimidating. This is the fear you need to deal with and put away; along with its cousin called *doubt.* Actor and movie producer David A. R. White said, *"If you allow fear to get in your way; to stop you from getting to where you want to be, you run the risk of a far less rewarding and fulfilling life than what could have been."*

So, do not settle for what is just safe or comfortable. Launch out, Take the risks, and go beyond the normal and predictable, even if you feel afraid or daunted. There are things that will make you nervous or fearful. There are things that will intimidate you. However, you have to decide that you are not going to allow fear and intimidation to stop you. Sometimes it is not about waiting for the fear to leave, but engaging in what you need to despite the present fear. Go ahead and do it, even if you are afraid. Joyce Meyer says, *"Do it afraid."* Challenge that unhealthy fear. Put it on the run.

The *positive fear* signifies a deep reference and respect for someone or something. There is a verse in the Bible that instructs people to fear the Lord. This does not suggest that people ought to be afraid of God in a negative sense. That word fear translated from Hebrew means reference and honour and awe. When you reference and honour God, this is the beginning of wisdom. Psalm 111:10 lets you and I know that those who honour and respect God have great understanding. The Hebrew word for fear is yarē (pronounced yaw-ray). It *means awe, admiration, honour, reference and respect.* Obeying God and walking in His ways is borne out of one's respect, honour and adoration of Him.

God does not force people to fear or be reverent of Him. Rather, He wants people's adoration and honour of Him to come from desirous and willing hearts. If one's heart is not in it, then actions and lip service are futile in Gods' eyes. A Scripture from the book of Deuteronomy sums it all up perfectly:

". . . What does the LORD your God require of you, but to fear the LORD your God, to walk in all His ways and to love Him, to serve the LORD your God with all your heart and with all your soul, and to keep the commandments of the LORD and His statutes which I command you today for your good" (Deuteronomy 10:12) NKJV.

For instance, fear of standing in the middle of the highway is sensible. This fear keeps you safe. Fear of touching a live wire pulsing with electricity is wise. That fear protects you from electrocution. Again, this fear is the positive one—the one you need. It is common sense and self-preservation. This keeps you from being a danger to yourself and to others.

Dealing with Hurt

As humans, we can experience hurt or pain physically, mentally and emotionally. People experience hurt and pain that is invisible to the physical eye. The hurts that are below the surface, in one's soul require special treatment. We have emotions or feelings, which can be bruised, impaired, and crippled.

How you progress after being hurt depends on how you respond to the attack. In some cases, healing can take longer, especially for deep-seated offences or pain. People can hurt you with their words or actions. The wise choice would be for you to remove yourself from situations or relationships that have the potential to harm you greatly.

Everyone has experienced hurt or pain in some way. No one is exempt. It is mainly because people love and care with their heart. It makes them susceptible to hurt. However, we can find ways to reduce the frequency or severity of the hurt or pain. You do not want repeated hurt by the very same things that hurt you in the past. People will offend you by what they do or do not do, but do not let those offences derail you from your course, for you are not without remedy or relief.

Comfort, love and peace become such wonderful friends to you to soothe you and lift those heavy weights and burdens. It is imperative that you deal with your heartaches, lest they threaten to hamper your progress as far as your dreams and aspirations are concerned. Get to the root cause. Acknowledge the hurt instead of ignoring it, or pretending it is not there. When you acknowledge it, you can then deal with it and get past it.

You may have to confront those who are causing you hurt. Smiling in their faces as if nothing is wrong will not make the hurt go away. Do not let things fester inside of you. If you do, you will become bitter and defensive, and ensuing unforgiveness is a soul-killer that will snatch from you your joy, peace and relationships.

Hurting people are likely to inflict hurt on others, even if they do not intentionally plan to. Sometimes people cannot tolerate the similar issues in the lives of others with which they themselves struggle. In stark contrast, those who experience healing and deliverance end up spreading healing and hope to others. A lesson learned, then: you cannot give what you do not have.

In the book of Genesis, chapters 40 through 46, there is a record of Joseph's suffering caused by his very own brothers. Their evil actions against him caused deep hurt, but when he came face to face with them many years later, he dealt with it. He then went on to forgive them, and even helped them greatly, using his political and economic power to save them from a devastating famine. He did not deny the pain, hurt and rejection meted out to him by those who were supposed to love and protect him. However, he decided to address it, let it go and move on with life. Joseph did not use his rise to power and his influence to harm his brothers. Many times, God uses the very things that hurt you to bless you and others. When you can turn your pain into gain (something useful and effective), you

are on your road to recovery and victory. God always c
use us positively to affect the lives of others, hence th
for His unique ability and willingness to heal the human soul.

Those close to you sometimes hurt you the most. It also makes it
harder to forgive, because you did not expect them to hurt you.
Joseph confronted his brothers regarding the deep hurt they
caused him, but he also forgave them. It made reconciliation
and restoration between them possible. Hurt should not lead
to bitterness, but rather be counteracted with healing and
restoration. You see, it was not Joseph's elevation that was
primarily instrumental in the fulfilment of his dreams—that
his brothers would bow to him—but his humility, self-sacrifice,
and ability to see past their evildoing. The same dreams that
filled the brothers with hate and anxiety ended up benefiting
them greatly. Let me make a pivotal statement here: No dream
ever benefits just the dreamer only. Your dreams are tied to the
success of others.

When you get hurt or experience pain caused by others, it can
make you bitter or angry, or cause you to wallow in self-pity.
Just as much as fear can, hurt, too, can cripple your progress.
You could end up putting up a wall of defence around your
heart. While your wall of protection attempts to keep pain and
hurt at bay, you also prevent the good from getting in. Not
everyone is out to hurt you. You need to open up your heart to
certain people who are there to comfort, heal and uplift you.

If you are wounded and bitter, you run the risk of stifling or
suffocating your creativity. If you are the cause of your own
hurt, accept it, deal with it, and learn from it. When others

hurt you, you will heal quicker by forgiving them. By forgiving them, you give yourself permission to move on, and to be free. It is not always easy to forgive, but it is necessary. The other aspect of this is to confront the issue with the person or people concerned. Confrontation does not have to result in a fight. It can lead to resolve, especially among work colleges, teammates or family members.

Hurt does not have to stay with you forever. Pain should not define your life. Allow your purpose to define your life. Many people convert their hurt or pain into fuel for their dreams. Chasing your dreams can be like a roller coaster ride. There will be changes, vicissitudes (contrasting or unpleasant circumstances), and positive and negative emotional fluctuations, but stay the course.

It is difficult to deal with hurt or pain that comes because of the death of someone you love. Give yourself time to mourn. It is understandable. I cried and mourned when my parents and three of my siblings passed away. Each death, each loss was devastating, and took time to overcome. Everyone needs love, comfort, hope and joy, because these soften the *harsh blows* of reality.

I had the honour of meeting Pastor Fiona Lynch from England at a conference in Dublin city in April 2017. She has such an incredible testimony of going from utter darkness, hopelessness, and abuse to a life in God's light, and newfound purpose. She tells her true story in her book: *From Darkness to Light.* She journals her life journey as a battle against abuse, prejudice, domestic violence, drugs and mental instability to finally break free through God's help, making a remarkable turn-around. She did not stay down and let pass hurts and pain dominate her life. Why did I tell you about Pastor Fiona Lynch? You see, everyone battling a dark and hopeless situation needs that glimpse of hope that they can have a better life; a transformation. Fiona's story makes it tangible, reachable, possible.

At some point, hurt and pain must become like scars. A scar says, "I was hurt. I was in pain. I suffered, but I am now healed. I see the scars, but I do not feel the pain." Some people have more scars than others, nevertheless, it is the healing part that matters most. Pastor Fiona talks about her painful past, but there is a smile on her face, because she has no pain, even though the memories are there. She experienced a new life of peace, joy and purpose.

The grip of pain and hurt will ease from your life as you continue to focus on the healing process. If there is anything you must leave behind, it is hurt. This is not to say you will never encounter hurt again. However, you will at least know how to deal with it. In addition, old, unresolved hurt will not compound new hurt. Some people are able to use past pain and hurts as motivation to pursue their dreams. For those who cannot, use the healing as motivation.

BEFORE ANYTHING ELSE, PREPARATION IS THE KEY TO SUCCESS.

-Alexander Graham Bell

CHAPTER 4

PREPARATION

Preparation is something that is crucial to most, if not all aspects of life. You have to prepare for a myriad of things in life, whether it is for work, school, parenting, a test, an interview, a new baby, a speech, or a party. Good preparation can save you from a lot of unnecessary chaos, confusion, failure and embarrassment. Benjamin Franklin said, *"By failing to prepare, you are preparing to fail."*

Preparation plays a huge part in making something work easier or successfully. In the preparation stage, you get to think, reason, and figure things out. You get to plan and evaluate. You get to test and try. You get to set things up. You get to find the best possible way. Abraham Lincoln said, *"Give me six hours to chop down a tree and I will spend the first four sharpening the axe."* That is smart preparation. The first four hours of preparing the axe makes chopping down the tree in the last two hours so much easier and certain. You do not have to sweat that much. When you prepare right, the task becomes more manageable.

Preparation is the *"act of getting ready* or *timely management of things in your life to affect a desired outcome."*

How ready are you for what you are about to do or produce? How ready are you for what you are about to birth in the next level or season? Interestingly, ants use the summer (present) season to get ready for the winter (coming) season. They do not get ready for winter in winter. It is too late then. Trying to get ready when you should already be ready is like opening the tap and then trying to find the bucket. Such poor preparation and indifference can lead to wastefulness and futility. It is possible to waste your life because you are not prepared.

Have you ever entered an exam room, knowing you have not prepared well enough for the exam? You go in sweating and nervous, thinking you have already failed the paper. Yet, if you have prepared yourself well, you walk into the exam room with confidence and with an expectation that you will achieve good results. You must prepare for success, not just expect it. Wishing for success without corresponding action will not produce success.

When I was a schoolteacher, I could tell which students had put in the time and preparation concerning an assignment. I could tell which students had researched and put much effort into the assignment. On the other hand, I could tell those who had not prepared or put much effort in. Most of my students realised that I would only accept well-presented and well-researched projects. These got the high marks. They realised that excellence was required. Good preparation leads to excellence. Poor or no preparation leads to incompetence, lethargy and missed opportunities.

Some of my former students always handed in assignments that were of a very high standard. They always researched thoroughly, and presented well-written assignments. Their assignments (content and visual presentation) were very impressive. They always scored the highest marks. They went the extra mile. Diligence is the key when it comes to your dreams and aspirations. Decide you are going to do it right: decently, orderly and excellently.

Aim to go beyond. No one gets significant recognition or reward for mediocre performances, because of poor preparation. If you desire outstanding results, go and prepare well. It is about going beyond the call of duty.

When an accomplished singer goes out on stage and belts out a flawless and captivating performance, it is a direct result of hard and repetitive practice. All the effort and preparation pays off. You will never do your best or look your best without preparation. That is why women take a little longer in front of the mirror. Taking a little longer will make it a whole lot better.

Many years ago, I did a T.V. advert for a company called *Game*. We spent over two hours preparing for this shoot. The actual scene lasted fourteen seconds. The director was happy with the first take, even though he took two more. The shoot went by smoothly and with ease because we had prepared well. A singer may perform on stage for a few minutes, but there were many hours spent in preparation.

A baby in its mother's womb is busy readying itself for life outside the womb. Proper and correct development while in the womb is crucial to the baby's survival outside the womb. Be patient with your developing, incubated dreams. There is going to be a birthing.

However, in 2016, my wife and I endured one of the most painful experiences. She suffered a miscarriage with our third child. Even though we had prepared and done all that was necessary for the development of the baby, something went wrong. Something we never expected. Then in 2017, the same happened. Talk about a double blow. This tragic experience left us deflated and bewildered. However, my wife and I gathered our strength and picked ourselves off the ground. Again, in January 2018, pregnant with twins, my wife suffered another miscarriage followed by another in December 2019. If there was any glimpse of light or hope, it was snuffed out. It felt like the door of life shut in our faces. Yet still, from the ashes of despair and pain, we found God to be an ever present help. We found the voice to utter praise to God and not blame. We had to continue living. We had to continue dreaming. Our resolve was in the fact that God knew all things, even if we did not. Instead of falling apart, we felt God hold us together as a family.

I call such unexpected situations *curve balls*. What do you do when life hands you a *curve ball*? A *curved ball* speaks of something that takes you by surprise, something you never expected. It knocks the wind out of you. It devastates you. Such things still shock us and leave us numb or bewildered, no matter how well we prepare for such conditions.

When one thinks about preparation, it is in terms of the good things. But do you know that Jesus' whole life on earth was a preparation for Him to die on the cross for the world? That was His central focus. No one wants to dwell on the subjects of death, loss, sickness or bankruptcy. However, one has to make certain contingencies. One has to make provisions for the unforeseen events or circumstances, whether pleasant or unpleasant. Many people will take out medical insurance or life insurance policies, and write out their wills.

On the more pleasant side, many save money for their retirement or holidays, or that special occasion. The question then has to be asked: what is the most important thing one has to prepare for? Have you prepared for where you will spend eternity? If you believe the Bible concerning Heaven and Hell, then you know that you have to make some choices. Most certainly, you do not want to end up in Hell, so you prepare for Heaven by accepting Jesus Christ as your Lord and Saviour. God made it that simple so that everyone can avail of this great offer.

Jesus himself knows how to prepare. His preparations were not just for himself, but for the entire human race too. In John 14:2, he said to His disciples,

"In My Father's house are many mansions; if it were not so, I would have told you. I go to prepare a place for you. And if I go and prepare a place for you, I will come again and receive you to Myself; that where I am, there you may be also" NKJV.

Heaven is preparing for you and me. Humans are not just important here on earth, but in Heaven as well. Parents prepare things in advance for their children. God does the same for you and me, because we are His children. God will not bring His children to an unprepared place. When God asked Moses to deliver the Israelites from Egypt, He told Moses He was leading the nation of Israel to Canaan. This was a place 'flowing with milk and honey'; a peaceful and fertile land, full of provision.

God never leads people into what He has not prepared for them; just as a teacher should not lead students into a lesson he or she has not prepared for, or does not fully understand. The same would be for a surgeon. Preparation is made prior to the patient's arrival in the operating room.

1 Corinthians. 2:9 says: *"Eye has not seen, nor ear heard, Nor have entered into the heart of man the things which God has prepared for those who love Him"* (NKJV).

When you are going on a trip or holiday, you prepare in advance for it. You secure a destination. You make travel arrangements and a spending budget. You put together an itinerary. You do all this to ensure a joyful holiday, not hindered by stress. Preparation makes things move along smoothly. Preparation allows for successful outcomes.

It is noticeable when you are ill-prepared for something. It hampers your performance. A polished performance requires good preparation. There are things in life that you cannot just show up to and do. For example, a music band will prepare months in advance for an upcoming concert. Students will need to study well before the test date. An actor will need to rehearse his or her lines for the play or audition in advance. Preparation affects delivery. Good preparation allows for a confident, precise and flawless delivery.

Michael Jackson's concert performances, including his music videos and dance moves, all appeared polished and dazzling. They had a distinctive touch of spectacularity. They were highly impressive, thrilling and sensational. This is because he was meticulous and particular, paying attention to even the minute details. Aiming to perfect his craft and do his utmost best, he pushed the pre-established limits and boundaries. Average was not in his vocabulary. When a person approaches their work, study, performance or presentation with such precision, it is nothing short of excellence and exceptionality.

Whenever I watch the Olympics, I am amazed at the ability, strength and excellence of the athletes. What you and I get to see is an exciting and polished performance, yet this is only the tip of the iceberg. These athletes have been preparing for years. They are serious and disciplined in their training, diet and general well-being. They know they have a goal to accomplish. They remain focused and immovable. They have already decided to pay the price. They are committed to making the necessary sacrifices.

Patience is important. Preparation requires it. Pace yourself. Do not rush too soon. Allow time for maturity. King David of Israel was anointed king at the age of fourteen. However, it was not until fifteen years later that he officially took the office of king. What was going on in those fifteen years? He was in preparation. He was gaining maturity through experience and service. During his preparation, he had to escape the assassination attempts of current King Saul, his predecessor. He had to learn to trust God. He had to learn to forgive and leave room for God to deal with his enemy. He had to learn how to command and encourage an army.

Know this, even though it costs nothing to dream, but bringing that dream to life and fulfilment will costs a great deal. You have to be prepared for this. Be prepared to put in your time, energy and resources where it matters. If other people invest in your dream more than you do, then I question to whom the dream really belongs. You should be making the greatest investment regarding your dreams. When potential investors see your passion, drive and focus concerning your dreams, they will invest in you. Apathy will hardly attract investors and supporters.

Whatever you value, you will prepare for. Before King David died, he prepared for the building of the temple of God. He did this because he valued the house of God and had a passion for worship. *"David said, "My son Solomon is still young and inexperienced. And since the Temple to be built for the Lord must be a magnificent structure, famous and glorious throughout the world, I will begin making preparations for it now.' So David collected vast amounts of building materials before his death."* (1 Chronicles 22:5, NKJV).

What are the things you value and how are you preparing for them to grow or flourish? Nelson Mandela had a dream. It was to see a united and democratic South Africa. His dream came at a great cost and sacrifice. Holding onto his dream with both long-suffering and undying patience during his twenty-seven years in prison revealed his passion, until one day that dream happened. The bonus and blessing of it all was when he became the first black president of South Africa. In prison, he had time to deal with bitterness, hate, anger, hurt, and any crippling emotion that would derail him from his dream. In fact, when Mandela was released from prison he said, *"As I walked toward my freedom, I knew if I didn't leave my bitterness and hatred behind, I'd still be in prison."*

Mandela was ready to leave behind the troubling things that could hamper his next step or season. In his season of freedom, he was already prepared to forgive and unite all the people of South Africa. His dream of democracy, peace and unity resonated throughout the world. It served as an inspiration for other nations and governments. Mandela was hailed as a true champion and icon for change, justice and equality. He prepared well by dealing with the things that had the potential to derail his dream. He called it his "Long Walk to Freedom." What kind of walk are you on, to champion the course of your life?

Action Plan

Whatever you are thinking about or dreaming about will never become a reality without an action plan. Without an action plan dreams will remain dreams, thoughts will remain thoughts and ideas will remain ideas. The fact that you can dream means you are capable of planning as well. What you need is the right kind of plan. You need a strategy. Having a plan is like designing a map for where you want to go, or for what you want to accomplish.

Short and life-long dreams are accomplished through planning. Builders need a floor plan or architectural drawing before they can embark on building that house or shopping complex. When you are about to travel to an unfamiliar place, you set your navigational system to guide you to that place. Things work better with a plan or map.

Having objectives or goals necessitates that you set some measurable targets. Goals are things you want to achieve or accomplish in a certain period. Put the things you dream of doing as a goal or endpoint. You must have something to aim at. If you have nothing to aim at, you will end up yielding to all kinds of distractions. Every year of your life ought to have a plan. In fact, you should have a plan for each day of your life.

Recognize which dreams have no definite endpoint or seasonal limit; and recognize those that have. Then develop and manage your plans accordingly to reach those goals. Do not squander your time because of a lack of planning. Readiness is important. December is a great time to reflect on the closing of that particular year, and then to look to the year ahead with fresh optics and desire.

Everything in your life needs a plan. A budget, whether weekly or monthly, is a plan of how you will spend your money. Not having a budget can lead to unnecessary mismanagement of your finance. The same applies to other aspects of your life.

A curriculum is a plan on how students will be educated through the year. A cleaning roster is a plan of how and when the place will be cleaned, and who will be doing it. These are just common ones. Some people's dreams are tied to their attending university or college. The realization of many dreams is in the daily progress that leads to the fulfilment of those dreams. You can make excuses and stagnate, or you can make progress and reach your goal or target.

You can put in place plans for the next day, week, month, year, decade, or century. Your plans can outlive you. King David in the Bible made plans for the construction of God's Temple. However, it was not him who built it, but his son Solomon. There are many businesses being managed or owned by people who did not start them. Many business owners have taken over their father or grandfather's business. The plan to start and run a business or some organization does not have to die with you. Even Jesus put a plan in place for His disciples before He ascended to Heaven. That plan of action is the Great Commission actioning them to evangelize the world concerning Salvation, and unveil the Kingdom of God to the world:

"And Jesus came and spoke to them, saying, 'All authority has been given to Me in Heaven and on earth. Go therefore and make disciples of all the nations, baptizing them in the name of the Father and of the Son and of the Holy Spirit, teaching them to observe all things that I have commanded you; and lo, I am with you always, even to the very end of the age'" (Matthew 28:18, NKJV).

You cannot have true success if your life is in chaos or disarray. You have to maintain a certain level of order and discipline. Even God does things decently and in order. The apostle Paul admonishes people along these same lines when he wrote, *"Let all things be done decently and in order"* (1 Corinthians 14:40, KJV).

Imagine if the planet had no order: no seasons; no water cycle; no laws to govern seedtime and harvest time. Imagine if there was no consistency with regard to the rising or setting of the sun or no consistency between day and night. Life would become devastatingly difficult very quickly. This all comes back to planning: ideas are not useful until there is a plan of action and logic order to make those ideas a reality and benefit.

Once plans are made, they have to be executed. If they are not carried out, they will remain on paper or in your head. Nothing will progress if you do not work your plans. Cameron. L. Morrissey said, "DREAMS DON'T WORK, UNLESS YOU WORK." What he meant was that you have a part to play in fulfilling your dreams. Your action plan is a vital ingredient in the actualization of your dreams and a vital function of management. Planning is part of preparation. Plans help you focus and stay on course. The plan or map will also help you know when you are off course.

If a business or organisation lacks planning, it will become chaotic or meaningless. Planning enables you to work it better. You are prepared when you have a plan of action. Businesses and companies plan things like staff meetings, board meetings, training seminars, marketing and many other functions of the business or organisation. Plans are adjusted as the needs of the business or organisation grow or change.

Planning eradicates wasting of talent or resources. Planning increases proficiency of the business or organisation. When you plan, you are setting goals in motion that you want to accomplish. Planning gives your dreams and goals shape and direction. When you plan your dreams, you show that you have faith in those dreams. You must also administer prayer to your plans, so you remain sensitive to God's leading and need for change or adjustment of your plans, if necessary. Remember that the Bible tells us to commit our plans to God and He will help us establish them (Proverbs 16:3). God wants you to plan. God actually trusts you to plan your goals. If you have no plan, God has nothing to help you direct.

When you plan, it will be either, a short-term goal, a mid-term goal or a long-term goal. Short-term goals are normally accomplished in a few hours or days or a week. Mid-term goals are normally accomplished in a few weeks or few months or even a year. Long-term goals are accomplished in a few years, or many years from the day of their inception.

Even God had plans. He did not just dream and stop there. He made plans to accomplish His dreams. He planned the earth and then carried out that plan. When Adam and Eve failed in the garden, God made new plans to right the mess. Failure did not stop God's original plan. What are you doing with your failed plan or plans? Deal with whatever disappointment you have over your failed plans. However, when you are done feeling disappointed, get up and make new plans. Your life is not over yet. Failed plans do not negate the rest of your existence on earth.

Planning showcases your professionalism and excellence. To say it another way, your excellence and professionalism is an indication that you have planned well; that you have prepared well. Planning is actually preparing for the accomplishment of your dream or goal. Mark Caine said, *"Meticulous planning will enable everything a person does to appear spontaneous."*

Plans can be good or evil. Some people plan the demise or downfall of others, whether through lies, deceit, schemes or traps. Satan planned to deceive Eve in the Garden of Eden and then carried out that evil plan. He succeeded when Adam and Eve accepted his plan. However, God had another plan. He brought Jesus to earth to die on a cross and crush the works or plans of Satan and to redeem humankind. God succeeded because millions accepted His plan of salvation. Ultimately God's plans prevail (Isaiah 14:27). People who plan evil against you will fall into their own traps (Psalm 141:9-10). God will preserve you. Trust in Him.

Understanding the Signs

Signs are crucial to life; for they assist in readying you for what is to come. A sign is a *mark or an indication. It is a pointer or cue to something.* Signage can also be *an act or show of authority.* Your signature on a document or contract is your agreement or acknowledgement of what is on the document. A signature can block or authorize, cancel or empower an action.

The word sign is the root of the Latin word: *signum,* meaning 'to mark', 'to symbolise', or 'indicate'. A sign conveys an idea, commands an action, or influences a decision. We get all kinds of signs, like hand signs, road signs, emotional (emoticon) signs, religious signs, or symbols. There are language signs. Sign language is such a beneficial tool of communication for those who were born deaf and dumb, or who have lost their speaking and hearing ability through an accident or impairment. This helps them to communicate their dreams and plans. If you understand the sign, you will understand the message. It is not just about seeing the sign, but interpreting it correctly. Your dream is a sign to something. Do not just see the dream, but understand it as well, in order to benefit from it.

Mothers know when their children have a fever. The most common sign is a high temperature. The cry of a baby alerts the mother to the child's need for food, comfort or a diaper change. The baby's cry is the sign, which the mother hears and sees, and then interprets in order to ascertain the baby's need.

A sad countenance is an indication that the person may be experiencing stress, loss or depression. People can say a lot without words. This is referred to as, body language. You can tell a lot just from a person's expression or demeanour. You can tell when someone's in love, excited, amused, sad, angry, lonely and disappointed; the list goes on.

When you are on a highway, heading somewhere, the signs help to direct you. If you need to exit at a certain junction, there will be signs well in advance. Have you ever tried to squeeze into a traffic lane, knowing you should have done so earlier? Ignoring or failing to respond to the sign could result in you missing the exit or turn. I cannot tell you the amount of times I missed a turn because of not paying close attention to the signs.

God gives people signs so they would not miss the wonderful things He has for them. God gives signs to warn, direct or draw people into things. There are signs that help to deter people from wrong actions. There are signs that help prevent accidents. Signs are not to hurt you, but assist and protect you as you live out you purpose.

Signs are like refreshing water to your parched throat when you are in unfamiliar territory. You welcome them. They give you a sense of where you are in relation to where you need to be. Sometimes you may be in a country where you do not know the language, but if you know and understand the signs, you can get by, to a certain extent.

If you interpret the signs correctly, it makes for a much smoother life. Jesus always spoke of the signs of the times. People know what to do or expect based on the signs. Jesus always marvelled (with disappointment and disbelief) at those who, even after discerning the signs, refused to prepare for what was coming. If you do not adhere to the signs or signals you receive, how will you advance in your purpose?

Each season requires certain actions and responses. Adapt and adopt to sustain your dreams through the unfavourable season until the next favourable season arrives. Do not let the season destroy your dreams due to your lack of preparation and discernment.

God actually made a covenant with Noah that He would never destroy the earth with a flood again. He set a rainbow in the sky as a token or sign of His promise to Noah and the rest of humanity. Every time you see a rainbow, it reminds you of that covenant or promise. Genesis 9:11-13 says:

> *"And I will establish my covenant with you; neither shall all flesh (human and other living creatures) be cut off any more by the waters of a flood; neither shall there anymore be a flood to destroy the earth. And God said, This is the token (sign) of the covenant which I make between me and you and every living creature that is with you, for perpetual (following) generations"* (KJV).

There is a wonderful connection between God, a rainbow and humanity. God made a wonderful promise of which the rainbow is the sign. God promised there would never again be a worldwide flood that kills every living thing.

Signs give information and they warn. A motorist refusing to adhere to a stop sign could cause an unnecessary accident. Many household products, especially detergents, have labels with signs and information. This is because the manufacturer does not want you to harm yourself, or use the product incorrectly. God gave the Bible as His manual to help mankind:

> ➢ To live the best way possible.
> ➢ Make the best of dreams and ideas.
> ➢ To live a full and satisfying life.
> ➢ To navigate wisely through the pitfalls and complexities of life.

Ignoring God's manual can lead to problems and detours that are otherwise avoidable. See the Bible as a sign book. It is a light to your path and a lamp to your feet (Psalm 119:105).

When a dog wags its tail, it is a sign that the dog is friendly. On the other hand, a dog that growls at you is signalling threat or tension. That then determines how you will respond. Your body has a built in mechanism that triggers *fight or flight* when confronted with a volatile or life-threatening situation. Your adrenaline kicks in, ensuring greater levels of oxygen to your muscles for a strong or high-energy reaction. It is instinctive. Your body is designed to read and interpret the signs, and then respond. The same applies to your soul (one's will, mind and emotions).

You may be wondering what signs have to do with your dreams? They have a great deal to do with them. Dreams themselves act like signs. They help to direct you along a certain path. They are an indication of your purpose and future. People can help direct you and advance your life when they discover what you love and are passionate about. When you only know your dream, it is like a symptom. A symptom is an inward condition only known to the patient, whereas a sign is apparent or visible. When you show or communicate your dream for others to see, it then becomes a sign.

When you are fatigued, it could be a sign that you are over-worked, or stressed out. It could signify that you need to slow down or take time off to unwind or re-cooperate. It could point to a medical need. You may be deficient in some element your body requires. When you feel uneasy about someone or something, it is a sign that you need to be cautious and alert.

When Jesus walked on water, healed people and taught them powerful messages, they were signs of His power and authority over creation. When someone walks into a room and gives orders to others, it is a sign that he or she is the boss or commander in charge. To put it another way, what you do is an indication of who you are in relation to your status or position.

In the Bible book of Exodus, Moses saw a bush on fire. However, the bush itself was not damaged or consumed by the fire. This sign caught his attention. He drew closer to observe this phenomenon. At that point, God spoke to him and redirected his life. The burning bush was just a sign to attract Moses' attention and change the course of his life. Every new level you aspire to will have signs along the way that help you transition to that next level.

When Moses agreed to go back to Egypt to be God's representative and commander for the Israelites, he asked

God for a sign. He did this because he wanted the Israelites to believe that God had sent him. This account is in Exodus 4:1-4:

"But suppose, they [the Israelites] will not believe me or listen to my voice; suppose they say, 'The LORD has not appeared to you.' So the LORD said to him, 'What is in your hand?' He [Moses] said, 'A rod.' And He said, 'Cast it on the ground.' So he cast it on the ground, and it became a serpent; and Moses fled from it. Then the LORD said to Moses, 'Reach out your hand and take it by the tail' [and he reached out his hand and caught it, and it became a rod again in his hand]" (NKJV).

This passage shows you that God gave Moses power and authority over nature, but that was not all, as the next passage reveals Moses receiving power over sickness:

"Furthermore the LORD said to him, 'Now put your hand in your bosom [chest]' And he put his hand in his bosom, and when he took it out, behold, his hand was leprous, like snow. And He [God] said, 'Put your hand in your bosom again.' So he put his hand in his bosom again, and drew it out of his bosom, and behold, it was restored like his other flesh" (Exodus 4: 6-7, NKJV).

He demonstrated this before the Israelites as a sign that God had sent him and was with him. God also gave Moses power to turn water to blood and then back to water. This is in Exodus 4:9:

"And it shall be, if they do not believe even these two signs, or listen to your voice, that you shall take water from the river and pour it on the dry land. The water which you take from the river will become blood on the dry land" (NKJV).

When Adam and Eve sinned in the Garden of Eden, God sacrificed an animal and clothed them with the skins. This was a sign of God's redemptive nature and foreshadowed the salvation that would come through Jesus Christ's death on the cross as a payment for mankind's sins. You can see how much God uses signs, as much as humans do. Always watch for signs, for they are purposeful.

Fruitfulness (Planting and Reaping)

Fruitfulness speaks of being productive and efficient with your gifts and abilities. It is that ability to take what seems less or insignificant and turn it into something great and meaningful. It is about increase and expansion. Fruitfulness brings fulfilment in life. Abundance is good.

Farmers understand all too well the importance of sowing in order to bring forth a harvest. A harvest begins with seed. To be fruitful, you will need to plant something. You must then cultivate what you plant so it grows and increases. Seeds, when planted germinate and produce. Seeds are the birthing place of fruitfulness. Your dreams are like seeds that you plant and nurture or cultivate to bring forth a great harvest in your life. Planting is part of preparation. Your dreams and ideas are seeds. Plant them, no matter how small.

Before a farmer sows seed, he clears and ploughs the ground to soften it and make it conducive for the seed. No farmer will plant seed on stony or infertile ground. That would be a waste of good seed. Sometimes things you desire do not manifest in your life because you did not deal with or remove the hindrances. Laziness, apathy, indifference, bitterness, fear, jealousy and procrastination are some of the things that hinder growth. Do not allow these things to choke your dreams. They are like weeds. Uproot them, even though they may be uncomfortable or painful.

People who become fruitful are people who have taken the effort and initiative to plant. Laziness will never bring in a harvest or bring out the best in you. Laziness is like someone sitting in a rocking chair that seems to have motion, but is actually going nowhere. God put dreams in your heart for you to make something of them, not just carry them about. Do not leave your dreams dormant. It takes work and dedication to make dreams a reality. Laziness will stall your dreams. Because of laziness or poor motivation, some people never finish what they start. They are robbing themselves of the sweet taste of victory and fulfilment.

Others may have more than you do, and accomplish more, but do not let it discourage you from doing your best with what you have. You are not commissioned to make happen what is in someone else's hand. Make something happen with what you have. God never asked Moses what was in someone else's hand, but his own. God wants to use what you possess and do great exploits in and through you with what you possess.

God designed humans to be fruitful. Hence, in John 15:8, Jesus encouraged His disciples to bear fruit:

> *"Herein is my Father glorified that*
> *you bear much fruit . . ."* (KJV).

Bearing much fruit requires action, dedication and consistency. Manifest the best in you by being productive with your dreams and ideas. Work at being fruitful. Colossians 1:10 says:

". . . be fruitful in every good work . . ." (KJV).

You do not want to be like a tree without fruit. A fruit tree is designed to produce fruit. If it does not, it has failed to live up to its purpose. If you do not produce fruit in your life, you are basically living a life with unfulfilled purpose. You do not want a bare and empty life. God put too much potential and ability in you for you not to manifest greatness. The survival and multiplication of the tree is in its fruit, because the seeds are in the fruit.

It is possible to be quite busy but not quite fruitful. This is not the best way to live your life. It is a waste of time to expend lots of energy or effort, but have no fruit from that effort. Be wise with your time. Do not let others keep you busy for their gain and your loss. You ought to profit from your expended time and energy.

Fruitfulness is not just a suggestive aspect of life, but rather an imperative one. It is necessary. It benefits you and others around you. In Genesis 12:1, God told Abraham that He would bless him and make him very fruitful, and then Abraham's fruitfulness would benefit the lives of others. Your fruitfulness, similarly, ought to better the lives of others.

Surround yourself with people who will accelerate your progress and celebrate your success. Find people who are not intimidated by your increase and influence. They are willing and happy to see you produce your best. Plus, your increase will spill over into their lives, enriching them.

HOW YOU MANAGE
YOURSELF AND DEAL
WITH STUFF IN YOUR LIFE
LARGELY DETERMINES THE
QUALITY OF YOUR LIFE.

-Darren L. Johnson

CHAPTER 5

LIFE MANAGEMENT

Management is one of the most vital aspects of life. It affects your personal and public life, your career, dreams and relationships. It is completely necessary at all levels of living. You have to develop the art of managing yourself effectively, and managing others in your care. If not, your life will become unbalanced.

People are capable of starting many things, but correct and effective management of those things will determine the outcome. Management is about maintaining things. It is about upkeep. It is keeping things running smoothly and efficiently to affect or guarantee a desired outcome. That is why almost all organizations and companies have managers. They are concerned with the day-to-day operational aspects of that company. They need competent people who will maintain the day-to-day running of their companies or organizations. The development, growth and success of the company or organization depend on how well it is managed.

From a business perspective, management is *"the organization and coordination of the activities of a business in order to achieve defined objectives."* Mary Parker Follet provides an alternate definition: management is *"the art of getting things done through people,"* and Henri Fayol defines management as *"the act or manner of managing."*

Managerial positions can be demanding and challenging. You have to be confident, flexible, responsible and dedicated. There is a lot you have to deal with or take into account as a manager. As a manager, you will get to bring teams of people together with different skill sets and knowledge to work together in order to achieve common goals. There is that constant managing of the day-to-day operations. Of course, there are rewards and benefits that come with managerial positions.

Letting too many things slip can cause major glitches in the company. You are hired to fulfil a certain role with all its given responsibilities. When you do not manage or do your job well, it amounts to poor management. No business, organization or company wants poor management. It can cause the company to run at a loss. It is one thing for a company to lose profits due to the economy down turn, but quite another because of bad management.

If a task is huge or daunting, perhaps you should break it down into smaller manageable parts. Some people are motivated by doing the difficult things first and leaving the easier and enjoyable things for last. That becomes their incentive or reward. Many times, things that seem insurmountable, become simple when broken down or better understood.

Part of effective management is to stay committed to the task. It is also to stay passionate about the task or goal ahead. Effective management reduces unnecessary stress and fatigue. Part of effective management is to know your limits and boundaries.

It is about knowing your strengths and weaknesses. You cannot do everything. This calls for you to prioritize. Smart managers pull together a team of people who will get the job done in the best possible way and make the organization look good.

For people whose job title does not spell 'manager,' it is possible that you will handle some form of management duty. Do not shy away from it. You can do it. You are capable. Most things seem difficult, until you do them. You are capable of learning new things. Do not be intimidated by those in higher positions than you are. Allow growth in your life from what they have to offer without devaluing yourself.

Self-management: Caring for You

Self-management is about taking responsibility for your behaviour and well-being. It is about exercising self-control in all situations. The aim of self-management is to help you make a success of your life. It helps bring stability and direction to your life. Be your very own best manager.

If you do not care for yourself, you cannot care for others effectively. Poor management of self cannot result in good management of other people or things. Burn out, apathy or just carelessness with your life and your purpose will greatly diminish your usefulness and productivity. Neither should you care more for others while neglecting to do the same for yourself. Do not feel guilty about taking care of yourself. Go ahead and pamper yourself often. Get some T.L.C.

Loving yourself and knowing that your Creator loves you and accepts you are key factors to inner peace and confidence. If you find it hard to love and accept yourself, perhaps because of having not been a recipient of much human love and acceptance, you will find it hard to love and accept others for who they are.

Part of living a successful life is to love yourself, love others and love what you do. Maya Angelou said, *"Success is liking yourself, liking what you do, and liking how you do it."* I agree wholeheartedly. What is the point of doing what you do, but totally hating it, or hating yourself? There has to be more things in your life you absolutely love to do, as opposed to things you hate doing, but have to. There has to be something in you that rises up and says, *"I like me. I enjoy what I do. I enjoy life."*

How you see yourself matters. How you feel about yourself matters. Feelings of low self-esteem and insecurity will hamper your progress in life. This then leads you to approach life as a victim instead of a victor. People, who think and feel victorious, end up acting victorious. You must care about the way you think, feel and perceive things, from the most basic to the most substantial. Thinking your best and feeling your best leads to a happy you. Do not leave it up to others to make you happy. Do not let chaos disturb your inner peace. Do not let people drag unnecessary drama into your life. Do not let others mess with your sanctuary of peace. Let the drama stay out there.

One person's rejection of you does not represent the entire human race, and it certainly does not reflect God's opinion of you. In God's eyes, you were worth the death of His Son Jesus. In God's eyes you are precious and loved. Focus more on the many people who love and accept you than the few who reject you.

If you feel stifled in the company of certain people, then perhaps you are in the wrong crowd. If you cannot be yourself, and have to pretend when in the company of certain people, then perhaps they are not the right company for you. Find those who love and accept your authenticity. Find those who will admonish you without making you feel small or insignificant, and who will genuinely encourage you, or praise your efforts.

Emotional stability is crucial. The key is not to let your emotions dictate your manner of life. It is then incumbent for me to say that you should not make decisions when you are emotionally unstable. You may live to regret decisions made in such manner. I think we all can attest to this. This is not to say you should be devoid of emotion when deciding. It just means you want to be in the right frame of mind and be emotionally stable and sensible when making important decisions. It helps to take some time to regroup your thoughts and allow your emotions to settle.

Everyone will need help at some point in life. Shouting, "I NEED HELP," should not be viewed as a weakness and an embarrassment. There are people there to support you in moments like this:

"Two are better than one, because they have a good reward for
their labour. For if they fall, one will lift up his companion.
But woe to him who is alone when he falls; for he has no
one to help him up" (Ecclesiastes 4:9-10, (NKJV).

It is up to you to accept help when you know you need it. There are numerous organizations and centres designed to assist you, whether it is a personal or family issue, career advice, or financial help. Everyone needs help from time to time. I have a few trustworthy people in my life I can talk to about some of my challenges and private issues. I know they have my best interest at heart, and will always give sound advice. It is unwise to open up your heart and sensitive issues to everyone. Be selective.

Staying confident and secure with who you are does help you overcome challenges and reach your desired goals. When others say, *"You cannot;"* you say, *'Yes, I can.'* Have confidence in yourself and the abilities God gave you. Have some resilience and tenacity. Do not allow anything to diminish your creativity and your importance. You may be loving, kind and caring, but you also need to be tough, confident and assertive. Do not let others force you to do things that go against your core values and beliefs. Stand up for what you believe. If it means standing alone, so be it. You are better off with authenticity and self-assertion than pretence and intimidation.

Your physical body requires certain things in order to function well. It requires nourishment, exercise and good rest. Treat yourself to some comforting and pleasurable things. Get that massage, that foot rub, that pedicure or manicure, that hairdo or designer outfit you have always wanted. Feel good, smell good and look good. Feel important because you are. Some people reduce themselves to the lowest common denominator. You are too unique and important to be labelled as common. God has never created anything common. All God's creatures are unique. Humans are the crown of God's creation.

God gave you a physical body. It is only right to care for it. Without it, you cannot exist on earth. The point of the matter is not to only start caring for your body when it malfunctions, but when it is doing well. Quit smoking while you are cancer free. Why smoke until you get a fatal smoking related disease, and then decide to quit. Why abuse alcohol until you end up needing a liver transplant? Prevention is far better than cure.

Your body cannot function at its optimum if you constantly abuse it with excessive junk food, alcohol, drugs or other harmful substances. A car that is used for a prolonged period without proper care and servicing will eventually give problems. Your body will grow old, however, do all you can to care for it, so it ages gracefully. Old age does not have to equal pain, sickness and disease. It does not have to equal total weakness and frailty.

Medicate yourself with positivity and optimism. Proverbs 12:13 says:

> *"A merry [happy] heart makes a cheerful countenance, But by sorrow of the heart the spirit is broken"* (NKJV).

Insulate yourself against things that seek to devour your inner peace, creativity and energy. Work at strengthening who you are. Do not over stretch yourself just to please others. Saying NO sometimes is healthy for your soul. Saying YES to a myriad of things will eventually result in stress, resentment and burnout. Guard against frustration, prolonged stress and strife. They are not good for your mind or body. They are poisonous to your system.

There are five, crucial things you ought to quit immediately. These are:

> ➤ Trying to please everybody—You never will.
> ➤ Putting yourself down—Self-condemnation kills creativity and confidence.
> ➤ Being afraid of change—Change will happen whether you like it or not. Learn to adapt and reposition yourself.
> ➤ Living in the past—The past is gone. Do not let it steal your present.
> ➤ Overthinking—Relax, unwind, calm your mind. Leave some things to rest. Quit mulling over them, especially the negative thoughts.

Trust God, He is still on the throne.

These things weigh negatively on your mind and body. When you care for your mental state, you are also caring for your body. They are connected. When it comes to managing yourself, have a holistic approach. Care for your spirit, soul (will, mind and emotions) and physical body. The apostle John said:

> *"Beloved, I pray that you may prosper in all things and be in health, just as your soul prospers"* (3 John 1:2, NKJV).

Your Space & Your Time

'Me Time' and 'My Space' have their place and benefit in my life. For one, I love being at home, in my own space, comfortable. I love being alone with my wife and children. Then there are other times I just love being alone with no one around. Then there are times I enjoy being in a crowd. Each has its place and benefit in my life. Some people do not like to be alone or still. Learn to embrace solitude. Get to know yourself.

Being alone affords you the opportunity for quiet time, reflection, or just relaxation. It is good to just 'chill' out. Taking time away from the busy workday or boardroom meeting can be rejuvenating. Sleep is a unique factor of life. It is a time when your whole being is centred in one place. Your body has a chance to heal, to rest and replenish.

In the Bible, the book of Ecclesiastes tells us that there is a time for everything under the sun. Often, many people make time for everything else; accept a good 'down time' or 'alone time.' Busyness without good rest will lead to breakdown or burnout. It will result in ill health.

The week that my father died, I was so tired, broken-hearted and stressed out, I had quite a severe panic attack. It felt like my body was shutting down. I actually thought I was going to die. Two of my brothers rushed me to the hospital. I remember hearing the doctor say to them, *"He has had a severe panic attack."* That is all I remembered. When I awoke, I had no clue who I was, or where I was, or what day of the week it was. When I saw my wife's face, as she bent over me, my temporary amnesia faded. She told me the doctor had given me a strong sedative that made me sleep for twenty-three hours. That is almost a day. I felt new, energized and calm. I felt so in touch with my whole being. I felt unpolluted. It was an amazing feeling of tranquillity in my soul. It was the best sleep I had ever had. I recommend long sleep, but not the panic attacks.

Plan regular 'down times.' They are good for your sanity. If you rob yourself of 'down time,' 'alone time' or sleep, you are robbing yourself of healthy living. For me, 'alone or down time' allow me to slow down. It is amazing what you get to notice when you slow down. You start to notice the little things in life that are often overlooked. Rest periods are great for your rejuvenation and creativity. Clarity of thought returns.

My wife knows me well. She is always telling me to slow down. I can become clumsy at times when I do things in a rush. I end up causing silly little accidents or overlooking things. Creativity works better when you are relaxed instead of tense and overworked.

Your 'down time' or 'alone time' is you spending time with yourself, not doing things for other people. As I have said previously, you should not feel guilty about spending time on yourself. Sometimes not doing anything is good. It is not a waste of time. Rest your body and rest your mind. Just because you never stop thinking, does not mean you cannot rest your mind. Sticking on soft music, or just closing your eyes for a while, or even watching a pleasant movie helps. You are in a more passive mode when you watch something on the television screen. Some people choose to go for a casual walk. This too is good to clear the mind and cause you to unwind.

You cannot possibly be everything to everyone, and neither can you be everywhere. You are not God. You have certain limitations. Respect those limits. When you feel stressed or burnt out, it is a sign for rest time. It may also be time to cut back on your activities. When your body is aching and tired, it is telling you to slow down and take a good rest. Ignoring these signs ends up leading to poor health.

Some people find it hard to unwind from a busy day out. It just takes things that help you to unwind. Find what works for you and practice resting. Your body repairs and replenishes itself properly when you are resting or asleep. Regular TLC (Tender Love & Care) is good for your physical body and emotions. Eventually unwinding becomes easier. I tend to look forward to my 'down time' as a reward, especially when I have had an intense or hectic day.

Managing Others

Tolerance is one of the most important things when it comes to managing people. Understanding people, and their wants and needs causes you to serve them better. In addition, the way you treat others will determine how effectively you are able to manage them. No one wants to be managed or supervised by people who do not care about them, or who are harsh and indifferent.

It is not just about the product, but the wellbeing of those producing the product. If you build people under you, you will eventually build your organization, business or ministry. People work better when they feel loved, cared for and valued. A good manager will ascertain the needs and abilities of those under his or her care.

Ask yourself this question: How do I want others to treat me? Treat them the way you want to be treated. The Bible admonishes us to adopt this mind-set.

"So then, in everything treat others the same way you want them to treat you . . ." (Matthew 7:12, AMP).

Starting at the bottom rung of the ladder in the company before becoming the manager or CEO has its benefits. You become more appreciative of those under you when you finally get to the top. You get to show understanding, care and empathy. When you have been where your staff is, you will better understand their desires, aspirations, frustrations and challenges. You will understand how the various aspects of the company work as a whole.

Sometimes you may feel like you are doing so much for people who do little for you, or who disregard your efforts. It is not so much about 'swimming the ocean' for people who would not even 'cross a bridge' for you. Rather, it is about remaining true to your character. That part of you that says, *"I am a helper. I love caring. I am loyal."*

Even though you may be in a position of management, the people under you have something to add to your life. I am called to manage my family. It is a great responsibility, meeting all the important needs in their lives. I have learned to love them, cherish them, work hard for them and praise them. They are too precious to be neglected. There are times, though, where I have to be reminded that my harsh tone of voice or behaviour can affect them negatively. I am not perfect, but I must do the best I can. I cannot spend most of my time on my career and neglect my family. I have to balance career and family.

My mentor, political leader, pastor, and dear friend Wayne Thring made this following statement: *"Many today leave their families behind in pursuit of success. They value careers and success more than they do family. These individuals get so far down the road of success, and family is so far behind that they just keep driving. As the family goes, so goes the church and as the church goes, so goes the nation. Reprioritize the importance of family."*

Every ambitious person should heed this wise statement. Find that balance between work and family, and even dreams and family. Do not be so caught up chasing your dreams that you neglect or lose your family. You would want to be surrounded by family if you were very sick or in hospital, not your dreams or career. If you were on your deathbed, it is family that you want around you. In managing your life, make sure family has its proper place. They should be high up on your priority list. Find ways to involve your family in your dreams, if possible.

Sometimes people only see your value and worth once you are gone. I want to see their value and praise them now. The same goes for my friends and acquaintances. They must be valued, praised and encouraged. I have no business destroying people in any way; and neither do you. Naturally, I gravitate toward helping and encouraging people. Managers ought to help people find solutions more than complain about problems.

You must understand that management is part of leadership. Those who lead have to manage to a certain degree. God called Moses to lead two million Jews. It meant he had to manage them. However, he did not do it alone. He appointed helpers, as advised by his father-in-law Jethro, otherwise his management of them would turn into a burden instead of a blessing.

Managing people is no small task. Moses had to know his strengths and weaknesses. He had to know his limits. He also had to know the strengths and weaknesses of those under his leadership. When you know strengths and weaknesses of those under you, you can help them improve. It is a bad character flaw to use the weaknesses and mistakes of those under you against them. You lose the respect, trust and support of those you betray or abuse.

Managers have to be clear, decisive and direct. This allows those under them to be confident and to understand what is required of them. Be open to ideas and change. Those under your management may have valuable ideas that may prove effective, if implemented. Managers ought to inspire and motivate those under them. Remember those under you have dreams too. Help them flame those dreams into reality.

When those under your management face challenges or discouragement, your reassurance and encouragement will help greatly. As a manager, be trustworthy and be approachable. Treat people with love and respect. They are human, not commodities. When dealing with people, use your heart, for that is from where love, care and respect flow.

It is important for managers to encourage and motivate, but to also, hold those under their care accountable. Get regular feedbacks, which will assist you in tweaking things for better performance from your team. Problems will arise, but good managers will employ various techniques to resolve them. Managers have to be team players, not lone rangers. Managers should accept advice, not only give it. Stay confident, but humble. Stay positive and strong, for your team will feed off what you put out. Your positive attitude and confidence in your team will reinforce and boost their productivity.

Growing in Wisdom

Wisdom is the main or principle thing in life (Proverbs 4:7). Therefore, do your best to get it and grow in it. A lack of wisdom can lead to stunted growth. When you associate with wise people, you become wise. A key Scripture from the Bible (Proverbs 13:20) says, *"He that walks [associates or keeps company] with the wise shall be wise; but a companion of fools shall be destroyed [ruined]"* (KJV).

Wisdom will cause you not to rush into things. I prefer to eat the banana when it is ripe and soft, not hard and bitter. Sometimes people rush into things that cause pain and bitterness. On the other hand, wisdom will help you not procrastinate when it is your time or season to engage. Many people are frustrated because they feel like they have not progressed in life. They feel stuck. This can be due to them not taking the golden opportunities that came their way. They were skilled on playing the *waiting game*, instead of performing. You cannot wait forever. At some point you have to engage.

You will learn more from listening and observing. What you have to say, you already know. Learn something new by listening attentively to others who speak wisely and knowledgeably. This will result in growth and increase. Glean from those who have succeeded in the areas you desire success.

Growth affects everyone. People grow physically, spiritually, emotionally and psychologically (mentally). Growth leads to change, and change can lead to growth. Change is inevitable. Like or hate it, it still happens. If you do not change, you will affect your growth negatively in various areas. To refuse change is to refuse growth. For example, a person who refuses education or knowledge will not be knowledgeable or skilled. That leads to stunted growth.

A simple illustration of growth leading to change is when a mother goes and buys a bigger size pair of shoes or clothing item for her child. The change of shoes or clothing is in direct relation to the growth of the child. Smoother transitions in life are brought about by synchronizing growth and change. To select gears smoothly, the clutch and gearbox have to be coordinated. When the clutch and gearbox and all its complex parts work well together, then smooth selection of the gears is possible. This results in purposeful momentum. Begin to align things in your life and see purposeful momentum.

You must work at bringing all the different aspects of your life into harmony with each other. Stability in your mind, soul and body leads to a wholesome person who can achieve things in a wholesome manner. I really believe that God wants people to enjoy their dreams, ideas and visions. He wants them to appreciate and relish the journey getting to the culmination of those dreams. It is like having sex. It is not just the climax, but it is about enjoying the whole journey that leads to that sweet and pleasurable climax. It is not just about eating to stay alive, but about enjoying the meal. It is about enjoying the flavours and taste.

God designed life for enjoyment. It is hard to enjoy life when you are overly stressed, worried, or too tired. Maybe you just need to let go of bitterness, grudges or even guilt. Maybe you just need to rest and recover. Take time to re-evaluate and re-cooperate.

Dressing for summer in a cold frosty winter is totally out of synch with the present reality. You are better off doing what the season requires in order to be effective in that season. Do what the season requires, instead of striving with the season, resulting in the stalling of your dreams. You must adopt and adapt.

Growth causes you to increase in understanding and wisdom. As you get older, you spend less time on things that are trivial and time wasting. Your inner biological clock sets off the urgency for the accomplishment of things that matter and are of value. Moses prayed wisely, when he implored the following of God:

> *"So teach us to number our days, That we may apply our hearts unto wisdom"* (Psalm 90:12, KJV).

Wisdom lets you know that you do not have all the time in the world. Some goals are time sensitive. Certain things are only done effectively in certain seasons. If you understand the season you are in, and its changes and demands, you will do whatever is required to get the best out of that season for your life.

If you constantly put off what needs to be done now, you become a procrastinator. Perpetual procrastination will hamper your progress. Just remember, you cannot produce more time.

Time does not wait for you to get it right; rather, you have to get it right in time, and make life decisions and changes in timely fashion. Hunter S. Thompson said, *"A man who procrastinates in choosing will inevitably have his choices made for him by circumstance."*

You have to learn to work with the changing seasons of life. You become limited in what you can do when you are old. So use your youth wisely. Accomplish more. Set yourself up for a great life in your mature years by investing now, if you are not already old. If you waste your youth, it will affect you negatively in your mature years. In the same breath, let me say that God can work miracles in a life that has had a troubled and tattered youth. Many older people are redeeming the time they lost as much as they can.

We live in a world where technology is constantly changing, and changing rapidly. It requires that we update our knowledge and understanding of current and future systems. You would not walk into a boardroom meeting with a video cassette to show or demonstrate your presentation. Firstly, I would be surprised if the company even has a video player (VCR). They are very outdated. Have you ever sat next to someone who pulled out a mobile phone with buttons and a tiny screen? They almost seem ancient in comparison to your touch screen mobile phone and its other modern features. If there is a tool to make the job easier, use it. It is all about being smart with your skill, energy, time and resources. The wheel does not have to be re-invented. It is already there. Use what is already there to enhance your productivity.

There are times when you have to correct wrong things in order to grow right. It means you must be willing to deal with the unsavoury things in your life. It means you have to be very honest with yourself, and what changes are required. When you know you are off course, then you have to make the necessary adjustments to get back on track. T.D Jakes said, *"You cannot correct what you will not confront."* People are creatures of habit. If you let the wrong things persist in your life, they will become habitual problems that may be hard to eradicate later on. You do not want to end up where you never intended to be. You certainly do not want your life to be like a garden with overgrown weeds.

If you cannot manage yourself without supervision or someone watching over you, you still have some growing up to do. No one manages God, because He is very good at managing himself. No one has to watch over Him to see if He will do what He says He will do, or to see if He would keep His promises. No one has to remind God about anything. No one can help God be God. That is why He is God all by Himself. When He created human beings, He desired for them to self-manage and function successfully. I do not need to dress my sons because they have grown or matured enough to do it themselves. They do not need my supervision in that area. They can self-manage. You gain greater levels of independence when you can self-manage well.

Proper and adequate self-management in an area is an indication that you have grown in that area. This is the reason why parents discipline their children. They want them to grow up right; they want them to manage themselves well. Trees need pruning; weeds need to be pulled out; plants are bedded in the right soil type, and are watered. It all speaks of creating an environment for growth and maturity and fruitfulness.

No one plants a seed and hopes it stays a seed. You plant for growth. It may start out as just a tiny shoot; but at least it is a shoot, signifying growth; signifying a change. At least you then know the seed and soil condition is good. You know the seed is doing what it is designed to do—GROW.

God did not create you to stay the way you started. Growth is expected. He does not want your dreams to stay in your head and heart. He wants you to live them. He wants you to fulfil your purpose and reach your destiny. You are like a planted seed. He wants you to unveil the greatness in you through the accomplishment of your dreams.

God wants you to use your acquired knowledge and understanding in a manner that benefits and enhances your life. Wisdom will prevent you from expending your energy and resources on things that are vain or futile. There is nothing worse than reaching the culmination or end of your life and regretting the paths you have taken. Re-evaluate your life (pertaining to your dreams and direction) at regular intervals. How happy are you with where you are and what you have achieved?

Developing Your Gifts

You cannot successfully develop a gift without first discovering or identifying it. Finding out what you are good at is a step in the right direction. What do you love to do? What do you gravitate towards? Every human being is born with gifts and talents deposited within them by God, the Creator. If you do not discover and develop your gifts, they will remain dormant.

Get around people who are skilled and perceptive at seeing and drawing out the potential in your life. It stirs me when I hear someone teach, act or sing, or see someone paint. That stirring is an indication that I am gifted similarly in these areas. Work at what you are gifted in. At some point, it will pay off. While the gifts of others may inspire you, do not neglect to put your gifts to use.

There are different gifts. Some people are gifted to sing, others to teach. Some are gifted to preach, others to administrate. Some are gifted to write, others to act. Some are gifted to work with their hands and others academically and analytically. Some are gifted as cooks, hairdressers or strategists. Some people are gifted to make you laugh. They are called comedians. The list is endless.

The right tools allow for the job to be done right. God has given everyone a set of gifts in order to accomplish certain tasks. How can a teacher teach effectively without his or her voice and understanding? How can a plumber or painter execute their job without suitable tools? How can a surgeon operate without the necessary medical equipment and other required mechanisms? In the same breath, how can you fulfil your purpose without tools? Your gifts and talents are your tools to work your dreams, which lead to the accomplishment of purpose.

Your dreams and abilities normally work hand in hand. I love music. When I was young, I dreamed of singing in a band and writing music and playing an instrument. For over five years,

I got to play and sing in a band, and I write my own songs. I also dreamed of becoming an author. I discovered I was gifted at writing. This is my fourth book. In my teen years at school, I loved helping fellow students with the subjects in which they struggled. That dream and desire to be a schoolteacher began to surface. I realized my gift to teach. I became a teacher and taught for nineteen years. God has also gifted me to motivate people.

Whatever you are dreaming of, trust that God has already gifted you in that arena. Look within and draw from that internal well. Wise teachers and coaches work to bring out and enhance what is already in their students.

In the Bible, the book of Proverbs 18:16, King Solomon said:

> *"A man's gift makes room for him, and brings him before great men"* (NKJV).

Your gifts and abilities will open doors for you. Your gifts elevate you and position you. Do not neglect them. Work on them; hone (sharpen, refine, perfect) them, and put them to good use. As I have said before, your gifts help you fulfil your dreams.

Never be intimidated by other people's gifts. You are unique. No two people are the same, even if they are gifted the same. Learn to enjoy and celebrate the talents of others without being jealous or feeling belittled by them. Others should inspire you, not irritate you or intimidate you. Trying to dim someone's light will not make yours shine brighter.

When I was young, I discovered some things about myself no one told me. Then there were certain areas of gifting in my life that other people or some situation triggered. Others will eventually recognize what you fail to discover about yourself. Take note of what people say or present to you. Additionally, many times, your ability to solve certain problems signals your area or areas of gifting.

Developing your gifts starts at a young age, if you are fortunate enough to have parents who recognize what you have. Practise is probably one of the most key factors in honing (refining or perfecting) your gifts and abilities. If it is a musical instrument or sport, a tutor or coach is helpful in getting you to progress further.

Parents must take note of what their kids gravitate towards. My oldest son used to bang on his mother's pots when he was four years old. I would watch him and smile, whereas my wife would get annoyed because he was ruining her pots. While my wife saw dented pots. I saw a dream. I saw a gift in its infantile stage. Through practice and tutoring, I saw my son's raw drumming gift transform into something amazing. He turned professional drummer at the age of eleven. Over the years, he has played drums for different church bands, as well as a youth band. My added joy stems from the fact that I have played guitar in one of the very same bands, where I get to enjoy my son's drumming.

Perhaps you are afraid to show your gifts. Perhaps you feel you are not good enough. Maybe you feel you are not able or skilled enough. Maybe you feel it is impossible. Eleanor Roosevelt said:

"You must do the thing you think you cannot do." Get the help you need, but do not quit on your gifts.

Developing Your Character

Another aspect of developing your gifts is to develop your character. While gifts position you, character gives you longevity. Longevity speaks of staying power or keeping power. Character keeps you in the position or status your gifts place you.

Many people's lives are not ruined by their gifts, but rather by their lack of good and stable character. You have to develop good ethics, morals and values. You have to garner traits like honesty, integrity, loyalty, excellence, punctuality, responsibility, determination, patience and commitment.

No one is perfect. Everyone is learning and growing. Do your best to live a private and public life that is above reproach. Whenever you mess up, due to a character flaw, just make the necessary corrections. Work on what is causing you to fail. Deal with your weak areas, while building your strengths. Weaknesses are like roadblocks. You have to overcome them to get ahead.

A lack of good character will cause you to make decisions and choices that can lead to your downfall. Bad character works against what you really desire to be or achieve. The good thing about character is that it can be altered. Developing good character requires work. You cannot wish to have good character, but rather work on developing good character.

Leaders and influential individuals must realize there is a younger generation watching them, and many will imitate them. Leaders and celebrities shape many people in their thinking and behaviour. It should not just be about how gifted people are, but how they manage themselves. It should also be about their character. The same passion and effort put in to develop one's gift should be matched when it comes to their character.

The more you become powerful and influential; you need good character to bring balance. You should remain tempered and humble, not conceited and prideful. As much as you value your life and importance, do focus on others too. Your level of humility allows you to be approachable. It allows you to think well of others. Humility is not about thinking less of yourself, but rather, thinking of yourself less.

People do better when they have strong inner morals and values. If you remain true to your core values and morals, you will build a life that is respectable, beneficial and rewarding. You will not bring your life into disrepute. The people you admire and value will define or shape your personal value system to a certain extent. This then necessitates that you choose wisely who you look up to. I believe every human being has something of value and benefit to offer the world. It is a matter of finding what it is and tapping into it, and not letting bad character obscure it.

Someone somewhere is influencing your character, whether you realize it or not. If you desire good character and values, you need to be influenced by people who display such values. Do not allow people with bad character to tarnish your values and character.

Character is a life-long factor in your life. You will work on it constantly, improving it. As I have said before, develop your character with the same passion and dedication you develop your gifts. Being highly skilled, and having the right character leads to a well-balanced and healthy life. This sentiment was echoed by Doctor Myles Munroe when he said, *"Character will govern and safeguard your life."*

Character is about doing the right thing, even when no one is watching. An important question to ask would be, "Do you want to just look good, or do you want to be good? Do you want to look successful or be successful? Do you want to look happy or be happy? Personally, I would rather be good, be successful and be happy.

Good character leads to good works, which in turn benefits others. While working on character, just remember no one is perfect. You will make mistakes; you will get things wrong. The key is to recognize your flaws and then make the necessary adjustments to re-align. You will be pleased to know that God offers you more help than all the critics who come against you when you flounder in character.

Living in the "Now"

When I was in school, we learned about tenses: Past, Present and Future. Everyone understands that one cannot literally live in the past or in the future, but only in the present or 'now.' While you are able to think or reflect on your past or draw from experiences, you can only operate in the present. There is no going back. What you have is the 'now' and the future. You can also think ahead into your future, but like the past, you cannot live there yet. However, you can dream, you can plan for what is to come. That is the beauty of your imagination. That is the beauty of dreaming. Your mind is able to take you where you cannot physically go yet.

There is no point in wallowing in your past or casting your life upon the future while suspending the present. When it comes down to it, all you have is 'now.' The 'now' leads to the future. Therefore, it makes perfect sense to live now in order to get to your future. Live there; act there; engage life there. Be present in the present. Be attentive in the present. Alice Morse Earle said, *"Yesterday is history. Tomorrow is a mystery. Today is a gift. That is why it is called the present."* That gift is yours. Use it and get the best out of it. Life is happening now, not yesterday or tomorrow. When today is gone, you cannot get it back.

Everyone wants a better tomorrow. That is great, but what are you doing today to better your future? Tomorrow is not promised to anyone. Therefore, make the best of today. If you remain focused or anxious about tomorrow, you just might miss the beauty, joy and opportunities of today. You might be focused on a tomorrow or future dream, but do enjoy the journey there. When I go on a road trip or holiday, I love taking scenic routes whenever possible, because I love to enjoy the journey there. A great destination but a miserable journey there is not my kind of thing. I doubt it's yours either.

Your daily input determines your yearly goal. You have to live daily, not just exist daily. Otherwise, you will be out of touch with life. Things change quickly in this modern world, so keep abreast of things. Keep your momentum. Do not let life pass you by or get ahead of you. Cease the best opportunities that present themselves to you. Continual procrastination will steal your opportunities. Even God worked on His daily goals (Genesis 1). Each day He put his plans into action. There was no procrastination.

Too many people are waiting and hoping to enjoy life in the future, while struggling and living a dull reality in the present. Fun, joy and adventure are not just for the future, but also for the 'now.' Abigail Thomas said, *"You're worried about how you will feel at the end of your life? What about now? Live right this minute. That's where the joy is at."*

You should not wish for what you do not have if it makes you forget or despise what you do have. Do not let anything produce dissatisfaction in you for the 'now.' Enjoy that old car while waiting for the new one. You may be waiting for warm summer days and bright sunshine, but do enjoy and get the best out of the present season. Gravitate towards the good things in the season in which you find yourself.

People always seem to be in a race to get somewhere. Slow down and enjoy the 'now.' When you do this, you will start to notice many beautiful things you previously missed. God wants you and I to enjoy moments in our lives and not just rush through them. Sporadic victory, success and joy are not God's idea of a full and blessed life for you. I know you will have setbacks and failings, but your ups ought to outweigh your downs.

Even though dreams are futuristic in nature, you still have to live in the present. Aim to enjoy the journey of your dreams, not just the fulfilment of them. Plan for tomorrow, but live in today. Fill your day with meaningful things in your life. Do not let your past or future absorb all your energy, while leaving you deflated in your present. You need your passion, energy and drive for the 'now.'

The Bible talks about God being a present help (Psalm 46:1). Notice, it does not say God is a *past help* or *future help*. He is a present help, meticulously involved in working all things together for our good right now. Obviously, God will be there when people need Him in the future; however, He is available right now. Jesus encouraged His disciples to live one day at a time. In Matthew 6:34, He said,

"So do not worry about tomorrow; for tomorrow will worry about itself. Each day has enough trouble of its own" (AMP).

Make the best of today, for after all, it is preparation for tomorrow. Distractions in life can steal your attention, if you allow them to. Some things do not need your focus and energy, namely things that drain you and add no profit or benefit to your life. It is possible to be consumed by worry and uncertainties of the future, and miss the beauty of the present. Be mindful of today.

To echo, busy is good, but sometimes a little quiet and calm will benefit you greatly. Have you ever just reclined and closed your eyes and thought of nothing in particular? Try it out. It is healthy for your mind and body. Relaxation is not a waste of time, but a necessary aspect of life. Jesus gives an invitation to those who are weary and burdened. He said,

"Come unto me, all you that labour and are heavy laden, and I will give you rest. Take my yoke upon you, and learn of me; for I am meek and lowly in heart: and you shall find rest for your souls. For my yoke is easy and my burden is light" (Matthew 11:28-30, NKJV).

Living in the present, thoughts from your past will bombard you; or thoughts about your future. Do not let these thoughts steal your mind from focusing on and seizing the day at hand. You can only live one day at a time. Worrying about tomorrow cannot change tomorrow. If your mind constantly wonders into the past or future, how can you really live properly in the present? There is a familiar saying: *"Worry is like a rocking chair. You are moving, but you are not going anywhere."*

Stay Grounded

Staying grounded is about humility and sobriety (dignity, honesty and truth). You have to know what you stand for, and for what you are willing to live or die. Nelson Mandela had a set of ideals he resolved to live by and die for, as reflected in the following statement: *"I have cherished the ideal of a democratic and free society in which all persons live together in harmony with equal opportunities. It is an ideal, which I hope to live for, and see realized. But, my Lord, if needs be, it is an ideal for which I am prepared to die."*

God created you with value and worth. You are important. With humility, you can hold an honest opinion of yourself, while also uplifting others. It is about considering the needs of others, not just your own. When you focus only on yourself all the time, it can produce selfishness. You need an outward look. Here is a powerful Bible Scripture that encompasses this idea:

"Let nothing be done through selfish ambition or vainglory [excessive pride]; but in lowliness [humility] of mind let each esteem another better than themselves. Look not every man on his own things; but every man also on the things of others" (Philippians 2:3-4, KJV).

When you are grounded, you do not mind associating with people of low status. This shows you value them as human beings, even if they are not wealthy, famous or powerful. When you value people and treat them with respect and dignity, they will support you. When you find yourself in a low place, they will gather around to lift you up. They will defend you.

People will readily support you and team up with you when they trust you. If you betray their trust, you run the risk of losing their input and support. Stephen R. Convey imparted fine words of wisdom on the subject of trust: *"Trust is the glue of life. It's the most essential ingredient in effective communication. It's the foundational principle that holds all relationships."*

You must preserve the boundaries and principles that govern your life and provide a base or foundation for you to build on. Do not trade them for things that look glorious but have no substance, and that may be harmful to you in the future. You are better off building your life slowly with honesty and integrity than with lies and compromise. Not everything that looks beautiful or attractive is necessarily beneficial.

Shortcuts are not always good. Some can lead to trouble and unnecessary pain. Not every process can be by-passed. It is about getting there the best and safest way than just the quickest but often times, perilous way. Proverbs 14:12 echoes this so well:

"There is a way that seems right to a man, But its end is the way of death" (NKJV). Enlist God's help in determining the right paths. Proverbs 3:6 says, *"In all your ways acknowledge Him [God], and He will direct your paths."*

Having a base or foundation is vital. You have something to fall back on. Your base should not be limited to things or structures, but people as well. People who are foundational in your life will help cushion and comfort you during harsh or tragic situations. They will lift you up and strengthen you when you are weak or discouraged. This is how God mainly helps you, through other people.

Grounded people do not chase after every hype, fad or event. They are willing to make calculated choices and decisions. They prefer to mature into things, instead of rushing or dashing into them. Obviously, there will be times in your life where quick decisions and actions will have to be taken. Do remember that life is not an emergency that you have to rush into. Rather, life is a gift to be explored and enjoyed.

There are certain things that should form the building blocks of your base or foundation: *Love, Peace, Humility, Grace, Honesty, Tolerance, Faith, Hope and Self-worth.* No matter what shakes or crumbles, keep these intact in your life. Even when you reach up and high, keep your feet planted on your firm foundation.

Never let fame, fortune or wealth steal your humility, integrity and authenticity.

Proverbs 15:21 says:

> *"A man of understanding walks uprightly*
> *[with integrity and dignity]"* (NKJV).

Take deeper roots so you can withstand the storms. If your roots do not grow down, how can you grow up effectively? Deeply rooted people do not mind the rain, for they know the sun will eventually shine. They do not mind the heavy storms, for they have secured a sure foundation, much like the house in Jesus' parable:

> *"And the rain fell, and the floods and torrents came, and the winds blew, and slammed against the house; yet it did not fall, because it had been founded on a rock"* (Matthew 7:25, AMP).

A wise builder will take the time to construct a firm foundation. If you ignore or do not build a firm foundation, you will end up risking progress, stability and success. When you are grounded, you are settled and firm. You are steadfast and unmoveable.

Each stage of life prepares for the next. Do not skip important stages. The foundation is the starting point for any building. Without this stage, you cannot build successfully. It will crumble when tested by the storms, winds and pressure. You can change many things in your life, but do not weaken or remove your foundation. You must take care of the things that give you stability. Do not compromise when it comes to the things that ground (stabilize) you.

With stability (a firm foundation), you can build anything, be it physical, spiritual or emotional. Some people only focus on building things that are outward, but fail to focus on building themselves inwardly. When you take the time to build a strong and balanced inner self, you will be better equipped to build and maintain outward things.

There are many foundational building blocks with which to build your life and dreams. Here are a few:

- ➢ HONESTY (be real, truthful and authentic)
- ➢ RESPECT (live with dignity and treat others with dignity)
- ➢ LOYALTY (be faithful and keep your word, as far as possible)
- ➢ CONSISTENCY (stay the course; finish what you start)
- ➢ TRUST (be reliable and accountable)
- ➢ CONFIDENCE (believe in your ability and purpose)
- ➢ INTEGRITY (be honourable, fair and sincere)
- ➢ PESERVERANCE (have the power and determination to continue)
- ➢ LOVE (give and receive love, for love builds and comforts)
- ➢ FAITH (trust God, and have a strong conviction and belief in who you are and what you hope to achieve)
- ➢ HOPE (stay inspired, and expect great things)

FIRST, I HAVE TO THANK
GOD FOR GIVING ME THE
GIFT THAT HE DID, AS WELL
AS A SECOND CHANCE
FOR A BETTER LIFE.

—Oksana Baiul

CHAPTER 6

SECOND CHANCE

Everyone deserves a second chance. This rings true, especially for those who have actually experienced what it means to have another chance, or whose lives would be over, had it not been for that second chance. Whether it is a chance to redo or fix something, or a chance to re-unite or redeem yourself, or a second chance from the clutches of death, these chances help you learn, grow and become better.

Apparently, God also believes in giving people second chances. In fact, He proved it by the sacrificial act of salvation when Jesus died for humanity on the cross. God will not let the dreams He placed in you die. He wants you empowered to fulfil those dreams. He is an up close and personal God who is highly interested and involved in human affairs, and as Psalm 46:1 says, He is a God who is willing to help:

> *"God is our refuge and strength, a very present help in time of trouble"* (KJV).

When you have failed at something the first time around, try again.

Failure should inspire you to find another way to win rather than quit. Some people treat failure as if it is the *angel of death*.

Failure is not the end, and failure does not have the last say. Do not bury your abilities just because things did not work out as you planned or expected. Find another way; find another opportunity. Go back to the starting point, if you must.

Losing and failing can be disheartening, but you must remain resolute in the belief that things will change for the better. If you let your hope and faith slip, then you have nothing on which to anchor your future expectations. You will become despondent and pessimistic about life. God did not create human beings to give up on life, but rather to thrive in life. *"Be fruitful and multiply,"* is the command God gave us.

Second chances are appreciated more when you know you have blown it. The first thing to do is not to write yourself off. Others may write you off, but you should not. So long as you have breath, you can turn things around for the good or better. You are destined for greatness, even when life has taken you on an unsavoury detour.

Detours should not sabotage your greatness. When you take a wrong turn, your navigational system will always recalibrate. It rectifies your mistake by finding another path that will still get you to your destination. It may take a little longer, but eventually you will get there. Even if you feel lost or have no clue where you are in life, your Sat Nav knows. Your job is to trust and follow. God knows exactly who you are, where you are and where you are heading. Trust Him to lead you. He always leads people the right way. One thing is certain; He will never lead you to destruction. God will never put His *signature* on things that are destructive to you. In Psalm 23:3, David said it this way:

"He [God] leads me in paths of righteousness . . ." (NKJV).

There will be times when you will have to repeat things, relearn things and re-master things. You are being equipped to deal with what knocked you down or hindered your momentum. That thing may have knocked you down the first time; but you will be stronger and wiser the second or even third time around. Do not lose heart or feel time is being wasted. Growing ahead is better than rushing ahead. A setback, disappointment or mistake should be an opportunity for reflection, observation and refocus. Never let setbacks bury your potential.

If you asked every person whether he or she needed a second chance in life, the answer would most definitely be 'YES.' Why do people need a second, third or even fourth chance? It is because people are not perfect; and they do not always get things right the first or even second time around. People learn and grow, and that requires time, patience, understanding, tolerance and support.

There will be times where you will be the one needing to give someone a second or even third chance. There will be times where your love, understanding and forgiveness will release others and cause them to move on in life. No one can live freely and happily while straddled with shame, guilt or regret. Do not stay frozen in a perpetual cycle of regret or hopelessness.

Rejection is not the answer for those who have messed up badly. A second chance gives hope to their situation. Rejection shuts people out and puts them down. People want to feel loved and accepted. The reason why people from all occupations and social class thronged Jesus was His love and compassion for them. He viewed the people like sheep without a shepherd. It is the Father-heart of God that empathises with the frailties of humanity. Hebrews 4:15 says:

"For we do not have a great High Priest [Jesus Christ] who cannot sympathize with our weaknesses, but was in all points tempted as we are, yet without sin. Let us therefore come boldly to the throne of grace, that we may obtain mercy and find grace to help in time of need" (NKJV).

Second chances allow you to say sorry, to put things right and to prove yourself again. Second chances tell people you are better than your past, better than your failure and better than your weakness. If you are the one receiving a second chance, do your best not to waste it. Put it to good use. Second chances will mean nothing if you keep doing the very thing that necessitated that second chance. At some point, you have to grow up. You have to change. You have to improve.

Every day brings you a second chance. Tomorrow is a second chance. It is a new day. You get to start again. Even God's mercies are new every morning (Lamentations 3:22-23). If your today was not fruitful or satisfying, you have tomorrow.

Take all the negatives of today and use them to develop a 'beautiful picture' for your tomorrow. It is easier to give second chances to people who you think deserve them. However, God gives second chances to people who do not necessarily deserve them. God's love and forgiveness toward people does not depend on whether they are worthy, but it is based on His mercy, grace and love for them.

Sometimes people are too hard on themselves. They refuse to let themselves off the hook, so to speak. They remain riddled with regrets and guilt. They find it difficult to let go or forgive themselves. Others may have already forgiven them, but they will not be entirely free if they hold things against themselves. Too often, self-imprisonment is a real and sad human condition in which many find themselves trapped. They imprison their minds, their hearts, their dreams and their potential.

Perhaps a second lease on life is one of the most treasured things to receive, because nothing else matters if you are on death's door. In the Bible in 2 Kings 20:1-11, King Hezekiah was sick to the point of death. God sent the prophet Isaiah to tell him to put his affairs in order for he was going to die. Hezekiah got on his knees and prayed, and cried out to God. He was looking for that second chance. God actually sent Isaiah back to tell Hezekiah that He had heard his prayer and would add fifteen years to his life. Hezekiah must have been elated and appreciative. Life is the greatest gift, so cherish it. Life itself is your start, and your dreams are the wheels that take you on the journey and bring you to your destiny.

Be determined to remove hindrances and keep pressing on. After almost drowning once, nearly shooting someone by accident, as well as two major car accidents, I really feel I have been blessed with second chances. It is a miracle I am still alive, and I plan to make the best of the rest of my life. I am so appreciative to be alive and well and in my right frame of mind. I am appreciative of the opportunities God has given me. I am appreciative of my family, my friends and my mentors.

Second chance is not a once off thing. As you progress through life, you will find that you need second chances in different areas of your life. Do not lose hope when you do not hit a target. Start again. Regroup, recalibrate. Have another go. Wonderful things can happen the second time around.

DON'T LET YOUR SETBACKS
SET YOU BACK IN LIFE.
SEE NEW OPPORTUNITIES
IN THE SETBACKS. IT'S
TIME TO COME BACK.

- Ricardo Erasmus

CHAPTER 7

FLYING WITHOUT WINGS

For me, 'flying without wings' speaks strongly of doing the impossible—overcoming those insurmountable challenges or obstacles. It is doing what negative people said you could never do or accomplish. It is the fortitude and attitude of not giving up. It is the place where you turn your "cannot" into "can."

An aeroplane cannot fly without wings. Its engines cannot do it alone. Your dreams are like the engines of an aeroplane, but they need the wings (opportunities and supporters) to flight them. So what do you do when it feels like you have no wings to fly your dreams in life? There is something wonderful and joyous that you will experience when your dreams do take flight; when you find hope, strength and newness of life and opportunities even in the broken, dark or strangest of places, as well as the providentially timed encounters with people whom your Creator affords you in life.

In 2017, I had the wonderful privilege of meeting Ricardo Erasmus, life coach, mentor and founder of Paradigm Shift Academy. We met in Wales through a friend Kevin Levingston. Kevin had met me earlier in Ireland on a number of occasions. He ended up telling Ricardo about me. He felt the need to connect us as he saw so many similarities and positive drive and energy in our lives. Since then, Ricardo and I have become like brothers. We have developed a close friendship and have such a positive influence on each other, and have collaborated on a few projects. We have done Youth Camps together. We have performed in music concerts together, recorded music together, and have enriched each other with our experiences. We have also encouraged each other through various challenges we have faced.

While developing the concepts for this chapter, I felt pressed and inspired to include Ricardo's story. His life story is a story of "flying without wings".

Ricardo Erasmus: FLYING WITHOUT WINGS

When Aubrey asked me if I would like to contribute to this chapter, it was an emphatic *yes* from me. The aim of this chapter is to encourage and inspire you to know that you too can fly without wings.

From a young age, I determined in my heart that I would be a positive role model and someone that the future generation could draw from as an encouragement and a mentor. Granted, these are not the most typical aspirations from one who grew up in a high-risk community called Mitchell's Plain, Beacon Valley in Cape Town, South Africa. It was a community known for gangsterism, high unemployment rates, high teenage pregnancies, and prevalent drug and alcohol abuse. Nevertheless, Beacon Valley was also known for its community spirit and support, like the proverb that says "it takes a village to raise a child"—a place where the neighbours could discipline or correct other children because of the collective value of respect.

In the community, there was also a lack of fathers in homes, meaning that many children were raised by single mothers, just like my siblings and me. This issue brought more stress and burdens to single parent families, creating vulnerability and lack of resources.

My father left when I was ten years old. I can still remember that day clearly. The two of us had driven back home from a fun-filled weekend away of bonding. When we got to the house I exited the car, and my dad told me to tell my mother that he would be back shortly, not knowing that he would be away for months on end. He became an absent father. My dad would come and visit us sporadically. There would be excitement on his arrival, only to be met with sadness when he left again without any promise of return. I was close to my dad. At first, I trusted him when he promised to return. However, as time passed without his return, my confidence in him diminished, and it left me disappointed and frustrated.

Fatherlessness left a gap in our lives. It left us unprotected, financially limited, and without physical and emotional support, especially for my sisters, who struggled with insecurity issues. They needed the love, support and protection of a father probably more than I did. My absent father failed to provide these.

Drug dealers took the place of the fathers, and they would recruit innocent young men to sell their drugs, and let them know that they would protect them and provide for them. Most of my friends became gangsters, with some ending up in prison and others losing their lives. It was a sad and scary reality.

In my home, I took the responsibility of helping my mother with my brother and three sisters. I tried to be a positive role model as well as a father figure to my siblings and cousins. My mother was and still is my role model. She taught us values and morals. She lived with this motto: *"I am not raising you for me, but I am raising you to impact the world."* With limited resources and space, we found our home congested with family and relatives who were in need of help. My mother had such a caring, kind and encouraging heart that she spent her life helping others succeed. Her influence rubbed off on me, and I found myself encouraging others, seeing the treasure in others and helping them succeed without wanting anything in return. I believe that if you can help the next person get to where they need to go in life, then help them, because you get to add value to their lives. You become like 'wings' to them to help them soar above debilitating circumstances and towards their dreams.

From as far back as my most formative years, it was my dream to become a pro soccer player. I'd come from a sporting background: my mother played netball; my dad played rugby and cycled; and my uncles all played soccer. When I was five years of age, one of my uncles taught me how to kick a soccer ball for the first time, a trivial banal gesture which would come to instil in me a sense of purpose and possibility. In primary school, I was selected to play for the school team and really enjoyed the experience. When I played, I did not have any worries. I felt free to express myself. The first time I really missed my dad was when I saw my friends' dads cheering them on and encouraging them. It was then that I knew the importance of having a father in my life. It was a painful and obvious void. Some of my friends would ask me where my dad was, and I would always answer with a lie: "He's working away from home." I thought that if I played well, maybe my dad would come and watch me, and maybe he would be proud of me.

When I graduated to high school, I joined the soccer team called Morgenster United. At the same time, I started to become interested in table tennis at the age of thirteen. I remember people saying to me that it was too late to start learning table tennis; normally you have to start at the age of eight. I determined to prove them wrong and see their baseless words fall to the floor. I started to devote myself to training and learning from my friend Daniel Ditta who, at the time, was the South African champion. We trained every day at the community centre in Beacon Valley. I improved so quickly that, in my first year, I made the Western Province County team to compete in the South African Schools Championship, and ended the tournament ranked eighth in the country. Two more seasons after that, I finished the championship securing sixth place and finally, I finished in second place.

Yet despite these successes, I then decided to walk away from table tennis to pursue my ultimate goal—that of being a soccer player. And sure enough, no sooner had I decided to stop playing table tennis then people began telling me to continue playing, thinking it could be my path forward. These were the very same people who hadn't believed in me the first time! And you can bet your hat that that wasn't the last time in my life that happened, either! Sometimes people can be fickle, and that is why it is important to follow your heart and pursue your dreams. It is not what people say, but what you believe that matters, and I believed sport was my only way to get out of my defeatist community, and in 2001 I became the first one in my family to fly on an aeroplane to different provinces in South Africa to compete. This was a thrilling and rewarding experience for me. It felt like my dream was taking flight.

I got selected for the school soccer team, meaning I had the privilege of playing with top athletes. Some of them went on to represent our national soccer team. In my first year, I was selected for our Western Province County team to compete in the South African Championships. I have to give credit to my friend Brandon "Brakkies" Truter, who believed in my ability when I did not. He played for a professional academy in Cape Town called Lightbody Santos.

One night he invited me to watch him play in a pre-season friendly match at Athlone Stadium. While the teams were readying themselves in the change rooms, I joined the crowded audience awaiting kick off. That night I did not know that it was going to be my opportunity for me to come out of my comfort zone. The team came out to warm up and after a while they returned to the changing room. Ten minutes later, Brakkies came to the stand and asked me if I would like to play. He explained that one of their players was stuck in traffic and Brakkies had asked the coach if I could play in his stead. Without thinking, I said, "No." I tried to make every excuse in the book and I remember Brakkies saying in a firm voice, *"I know you don't believe in yourself, but do this for me, because I believe in your ability."* Immediately all my fears and insecurity left me. Brakkies encouraged me just to go out there, enjoy the game, and not feel pressured at all. *"Seize the moment and take the opportunity,"* were his last words, before we got into the changing room.

Brakkies introduced me to the coach, who gave me a kit, skin pads, and boots. I sat on the bench and in the second half with thirty minutes left in the game; I was let on to the pitch. That night I played against Benni McCarthy, who at the time was the future soccer star. After the match, the coach, obviously impressed with my performance, came to me to ask if I played for any team. On responding with a no, he asked me if I would like to play for his team, Santos. My response was an emphatic "Yes!"—a far cry from my earlier crippling hesitation. My excitement was through the roof because professional academies normally have three-to-four-week trials, and I played thirty minutes and got offered a place. What a great opportunity! I am always eternally grateful to Brandon "Brakkies" Truter.

From me going to watch my friend play to going home playing for the same team was amazing. I felt that the only way was upwards from then on. We played together in the league and we played semi pro together. In 2002, I played in a community soccer tournament, not knowing that it would be my last day playing competitively. One of the opposing players broke my ankle and that was MY DREAM CRUSHED. I was out of action for eight months, not knowing if I would ever be playing again. I was devastated, depressed and wanted to take my own life because of all the disappointments. Yes, I truly and strongly considered suicide—a dark and bitter time in my life.

I remember continually thinking, "Why me?" They say that hard work always pays off. I thought to myself, "I put the work in and all I get in return is a broken ankle?!" Feeling so defeated and unfairly cut off from my dream, I tore all my soccer posters off the wall. I did not want to watch soccer live or on TV. You see, I had poured my whole life into soccer, hoping to make it in the pro ranks, to help my mother and family. This was the toughest time in my life.

In 2003 a former coach, Mr Natys, came to my house to ask me if I would like to play for his team. I refused his offer. He would come to my house regularly and nag me to play, reasoning that I had nothing to lose. He wanted me to play in the Coke Cola Cup tournament. I eventually agreed just to get him off my back. I started training with them for the quarterfinals onwards. Sometimes people come our way to help us to reach our dreams. They come along to inflate our deflated dreams. They come to help set us up for a comeback. Mr Natys succeeded in causing my deflated dream to rise again.

We won the match in the semi-finals. I scored the winning goal, and in the finals, I scored the winning penalty on the same Athlone Stadium where I'd gotten scouted. Leeds Lentegeur, a non-league team, won the cup. After winning the cup, I never went back to playing soccer. I discovered that my purpose was never to become a pro soccer player, but to become a life coach and mentor to people, especially helping youth, students and sports athletes. I learned from Mr Natys about helping others achieve their dreams. I got to do this on a daily basis in my current career.

This new calling led me to become the first in my family to travel internationally: the USA, England, and Wales, where

I currently live. In 2004-2006, I worked at a summer camp called Camp Wonderland in Boston Massachusetts, as a camp counsellor with young people, where I met Bill Rollins, who became a father figure in my life. Bill was the music director at camp. When we met, I instantly felt a connection of safety and encouragement. He started spending time with me every day, and on our breaks, he would invite me to his house to meet his family. The right people will come alongside us when we stay consistent.

Having not had a male role model in my life for so long, I was overwhelmed by Bill's kindness. After camp ended, I flew back to Cape Town, where Bill would come to visit me months later to see where I grew up and to meet my family and friends. I began to feel secure and confident having Bill in my life. He became like a father figure in my life.

When we just take a single step daily, we will eventually get to our destination. In my final year of camp, a friend of mine shared with me about a sports ministry in the Rhondda Valleys South Wales UK. I knew that I still wanted to give back to sports even though I stopped playing. She gave me the contact details and I emailed Phil Davies to show my interest. I knew in my heart that this would be the next chapter of my life. Things were beginning to fall into place regarding my purpose.

I then met Elroy Duckitt, a fellow South African and experienced training programme manager. He was one of the first Sporting Marvels. Elroy is originally from Cape Town, he was asked by Phil Davies to interview me, to see if I was the right fit. He was such a warm, kind-hearted guy who made me feel so encouraged. Ten minutes after the interview, he closed all his files and asked me to share my heart with him. I shared about my upbringing, my disappointments, my dreams and aspirations, and my desire to help others. After hearing my heart, he excused himself in order to make a phone call, only to briskly return to let me know that I had gotten accepted as a Sporting Marvel. I flew to Wales in 2007 to work with an organization called Sporting Marvels as a community development officer, helping youth develop character through sports. I could not believe it! Unsurprisingly, he was promptly added to the by-then ever-expanding array of mighty men who encouraged me to follow my dreams

Yet his greatest significance in my life went far beyond a job interview. Elroy is also the reason I met my wife, whom I married in August 2010. My wife knew him when she was nineteen years old as a student at Cardiff University. He came to speak at her church, and he invited her into his friendship circle. Sometimes the right people will come our way to help us move closer to our dreams. Elroy passed away in 2021 at the age of forty-one. I am eternally grateful to Elroy and his sacrificial contribution to my life and dream.

And, of course, another person that I met in this amazing life journey of mine who is deserving of utmost credit is Aubrey Morris, the author of this very book you are reading. The day our friends Kevin and Leah connected us was one of most exciting times. On a few occasions Kevin had said to me, "Ricardo, you will love Aubrey." The first time Aubrey and I met, we instantly connected. We had similar personalities, energy and drive. We both came from disadvantaged backgrounds and were making the best of our lives and abilities. We both loved helping others. We both loved music and writing.

Aubrey invited me over to Ireland to speak at youth camps and conferences. We started encouraging each other and his family has become my family. In view of my humble beginnings, as well as all the times I felt so lost or hopeless, it is just such an overwhelming honour to feature in this amazing book about persevering until you've achieved your goals. Consequently, Aubrey has stirred up a dormant dream in my heart to be an author. Thank you, Aubrey, for this opportunity and for helping me see that becoming an author myself is very possible.

In closing, we all have dreams inside of us. Be faithful with the little things. Do not despise the days of small beginnings. Sometimes within failure, you can find purpose. Always remember that your pain has purpose. Who would have known that that boy that grew up in a high-risk community on the Cape Flats would come to have his own Transformational Life Coaching and Mentoring business, helping the community— now that is "Flying Without Wings."

Your internal dream is greater than your external circumstances, and your past should not dictate your future. Sometimes our environment and the naysayers want to dictate that we will be another negative statistic, and that we will not be able to be a positive role model or influence in our community, or the world, for that matter. I hope that this has encouraged and inspired you. "Flying without wings" means seeing the impossible becoming possible, against all odds, and still having an attitude of never giving up. Never give up on your dreams. Remember that you can FLY WITHOUT WINGS!

Aubrey Morris: FLYING WITHOUT WINGS.

Before I tell you about my story, let me quote two verses from the song: Flying Without Wings written by Wayne Anthony Hector and Steven McCutcheon:

"Everybody's looking for that something
One thing that makes it all complete
You'll find it in the strangest places
Places you never knew it could be.

So impossible as they may seem
You've got to fight for every dream
'Cause who's to know
Which one you let go
Would have made you complete."

I want you to know that if you have a dream, you have possibilities. Many people do not see the possibilities because they ignore, bury or give up on their dream after being let down by life's circumstances. They feel their wings are gone. As long as you have life, you can still fly.

I am the son of Thomas and Elizabeth Morris, born in Durban South Africa. To be more specific, I was born at home in Mariannhill, a place on the outskirts of Pinetown and the main city of Durban, on the east coast. My grandma, a former midwife, delivered me. The ambulance was on its way, but my mum told me I must have been in a hurry to exit the womb and take on the real world. Most of my siblings were reluctantly weaned off the bottle or breast. My mum told me I actually threw my milk bottle away when I turned one. No more baby food. I was ready for steak.

We were a large family of thirteen children. I am the middle child. They say the middle child gets to fly under the radar, as parents are preoccupied with the eldest sibling and the youngest. Not always true, as I can still remember the whippings I got!

My grandma was very fond of me. Apparently, I was her favourite grandchild. It was obvious to my parents and siblings. I was like Joseph in the Bible with the coat of many colours. My grandma lived on the same property as my family, along with one of my uncles. Nearly every day, she had me in her kitchen or living space. She would tell me stories, prepare meals for me and slip me money every so often. I loved it. At times, I would use her strong affection for me to my advantage. If my grandma heard me crying or receiving a beating, she would shout and come to my rescue.

As we got older, our family experienced a tragic loss. My younger sister Tracey died in a tragic road accident. I was eleven at the time and she was ten. It left our family shattered. It was the amazing love, encouragement and faith of my grandma that comforted us and pulled us together as a family. We would spend time praying together as a family, something we never really did before.

My grandma was originally from Swaziland, a landlocked country in South Africa. She used to be a princess. Swaziland is a bit like England. They have a queen and a king. I guess there must be royal blood in me. After the death of my grandpa, my grandma moved to South Africa when my dad and his siblings were still young.

As a family, we experienced sporadic periods of success financially, but most times we endured poverty and lack. I remember nights without food. I remember sitting for several exam papers on an empty stomach. This happened most times when my dad was unemployed. My siblings and I would make our own toys and come up with ideas for recreational activities. Sometimes we would watch aeroplanes fly over our house. They would be high up in the sky. I would always wonder what it was like, thinking I would never get that experience, coming from a family that struggled with the provision of basic needs like food and clothing. However, years later I got to experience flying. And not just in South Africa, but to England, Wales and Ireland where I currently reside.

I had one pair of shoes for school. At home, we went barefooted. The amount of injuries we incurred from this makes me wonder how we all still have all our toes intact.

For many years, I used to sleep on the floor. I got my first bed at the age of seventeen. It felt amazing. I was so excited I told all my friends. You can imagine the comments and teasing I got. New clothes were a luxury that came once in a while. Hand-me-downs was the system of keeping us clothed. My parents figured they would have to rob a bank to clothe thirteen growing children, let alone provide thirty-six meals a day.

My parents were committed to us, even when they had little to offer. They were hard working, and taught us values and principles that have helped shape our lives to this day. When my parents had major relationship issues, my siblings and I feared we would be torn apart as a family. Yet amazingly, my parents stayed together through the highs and lows.

There were many fun times, like trips to the beach or travelling to visit extended family. I use to enjoy sitting with my twelve siblings around the fire at night, telling stories and jokes. Alas, some days were filled with teasing and fighting as well. My mum was patient, but my short-tempered dad kept us in line.

I used to study and do my homework in poor candle light, as we had no electricity, and no running water. My older brothers would fetch water from one of our neighbours. There were times I would end up with candle wax on my books. Some nasty class mates would make fun of that. I felt hurt and embarrassed. Yet my academic results were excellent. Some of my friends would get me to teach them and help them with the subjects or concepts they struggled in. Some of my class mates started calling me 'doctor.'

When I completed high school, I had no finances to pursue further education. I wanted to be an engineer or teacher. In addition, I had an interest in music and writing. Unfortunately, I had no money for university. I felt sad that I could not capitalize on my excellent high school grades. I felt like I had worked so hard, scooping up all the awards at the awards ceremony

(Matric or Debs Ball), only to end up with some menial job that did not match my educational abilities and talents. I felt directionless. However, my high school secretary, Mrs Goss, presented an amazing opportunity to me. She saw a somewhat depressed and frustrated eighteen-year-old who had dreams but no way to flight them. She helped me secure, what they called back then, a bursary (government student funding for teachers) to pay for university studies, and the bonus was that I would not have to pay back the bursary, provided I taught for four years in a government school.

Through Mrs Goss's efforts of sorting my applications and liaising with various departments, I landed a place at Edgewood University where I completed a four-year teacher-training course. I graduated in 1996 and began a career as an educator in South Africa. My dream as a teacher had materialized. I was flying without wings.

In my first year of university, I dabbled in drugs even though I knew it was not good for me. Meeting a father figure, church pastor and member of parliament, none other than Mr Wayne Thring, was a lifeline. He became a positive role model and influence that stabilized me and made me determined to live a sober and purposeful life. Wayne Thring also played a positive and strategic role in my whole family. It was an honour to have him endorse two of my previous books. Even to this day, he remains my friend, mentor, encourager, spiritual adviser and father figure. We all need someone like this in our lives. Every time I visit South Africa, we always enjoy fellowship with him and his family. By the way, his wife Leona Thring is such a sweet, creative, and faith-filled person, and of course, an amazing cook.

While at university, in my third year, my mother passed away. It left me and my siblings devastated. Mum was a pillar and our world. Everything felt hopeless. However, we pulled through and pressed on with life. Things come along and knock the wind out of your sails. Nevertheless, winds of hope and courage will blow again, to give you momentum.

At university I met a fellow student Timothy David, who became such a good friend. He had a small van, and used to lift me to university and back home. He would even bring extra lunch for me when he discovered I was too poor to afford lunch. He also introduced me to his whole family who resided in Petermaritzburg, a large town approximately forty-five minutes from my home town. During the week Timothy stayed with his relatives, and would go home on weekends. Sometimes he took me to stay at his house. His whole family were so good to me. Whenever I visit South Africa, I always dropped in to see his parents.

In my early years of employment, I would assist my struggling family and younger siblings, trying to follow the example of some of my older siblings before they married and moved on. My other dream was to help youth, so I formed a youth organization called the ACC (Addington Christian Club), where a few teachers and myself used youth building programmes and retreats to bring spiritual direction, hope, joy and stability to youth. I also had other youth activities in my community.

The week I was to immigrate to Ireland in 2005, my ticket was not paid for due to financial complications from one of my brothers who was already residing in Ireland. While wondering what to do, and feeling as though I was in limbo, having already resigned from my previous school (not to mention all the concerns of the needs of my wife and two children, along with several bills) I received a call from one of my close friends. Richard Beeson and I had met at university and become such good friends that he was like a brother to me. We ended up forming a rap group called A4J and we would sing and rap at church concerts and on the beachfront.

Richard had moved back to England with his family, having grown up in South Africa for many years. His phone call was so important to the next phase of my life and purpose, that, to this day I still marvel. To cut a long story short, Richard wanted to know how I was doing. I mentioned that I was leaving for Ireland. He then asked if I had my plane ticket sorted. Bear in mind, he had no idea I was ticketless. I lied and said it was sorted. The next day Richard calls back and presses me about my flight. After telling him the truth—that my brother could not buy my plane ticket, and had been too embarrassed to tell me—Richard offered to pay. He ignored my refusal and bought the plane ticket. That is how I arrived in Ireland in August 2005. I thought I was not going to fly, but by God's grace and providence, Richard was the catalyst to make my flight possible. Then I realized that meeting him back at university had been divinely ordained and orchestrated.

There are many other people, friends, and acquaintances whom I have partnered with in a meaningful and dream-building way. In 2008 I met Gerard Chimbganda at a wedding I hosted. We clicked and over the years became like brothers. Gerard is a business owner and church pastor. He has been such an encouragement to me and my family through the years. On one particular occasion, when I had a major issue with my residency in Ireland, which would have seen me having to leave Ireland and return to South Africa, it was Gerard and the important people he knew in immigration that helped to resolve my issues. Without him, I would probably not be in Ireland today, and you might not be reading this book.

In response, I have always tried to find people who have a need and help them meet that need or encourage and fund their dream. We have to be givers and not just takers or receivers. I have to help others flight their dreams as much as I have been helped.

In 2015, I took a great risk by leaving my day job. For a year, I took a few courses and had two job offers as a teacher in England. But I did not sense that release or peace about moving to England. So I developed a business idea (one of my other dreams of being a painter and decorator). I can remember in my second year, wondering if I should quit when the business was not doing well, and felt like it was not taking flight. Nevertheless, with the encouragement of my wife, I persevered with diligence and excellence. By the third year, my business began to flourish. By the fifth year, my profits had nearly doubled as compared to my third and fourth year. It feels satisfying and exciting to see the success of my business that I started with very limited resources.

From the age of twelve, I developed a strong desire for books and movies and novels. I would read at least four books a month. I also loved drama and acting. I carried in my heart a dream of one day becoming an author, an actor, and a screenplay writer. It seemed far-fetched and impossible in the past, but to date, I have authored four books, written several school plays, and scripted a number of plays for my youth groups.

I also decided to attend acting classes and drama school, and had the wonderful privilege of being on movie sets in small roles. One particularly thrilling experience that comes to mind is when I met popular Irish director Frank Berry, as well as Josh O'Connor (British actor known for his portrayal of young Prince Charles in the Netflix drama The Crown), and Leticia Wright from *Black Panther*. Like mine, your dream might start small, but at least it starts.

In 2019, I attended acting classes at Dublin Central School of Acting run by casting director Gillian Reynolds. I had done three other similar courses at the Gaiety Theatre, but wanted to brush up on my skills. I learnt so much from Gillian's brilliant course. This is where I met Caroline Quinn, who at the time was a film student at Maynooth University. Her skills and creativity sparked ideas and passion in me to pursue filmmaking and script writing. She has also shared with me some of her own scripts. We collaborated and put into production one of my scripts, and my first short film called "The Final Goodbye" was created. She brought great skill and creativity to the production of this script. I think she is becoming an awesome film director and writer. It is good to collaborate with those who have similar passions and ideas as yourself. It can only enrich your life and goals.

When Caroline needed a lead character for her short film, she offered me the role. The experience was great. Talking with Caroline, I sensed that there was so much more we could achieve when we collaborate with strategic people who come into our lives. We must cherish the people we meet, for we never know how strategic and life-impacting they will become to our future dreams and assist in helping us fulfil our purpose. I guess in some way, we are all here to help each other fly without wings. In other words, we become the wings that help flight their dreams.

My story is still being written. There are new, exciting chapters to come, and the same is true for you. Your life and dreams matter. Let your story (life and dreams) inspire others.

ONE WAY TO GET THE
MOST OUT OF LIFE IS
TO LOOK UPON IT AS
AN ADVENTURE.

- William Feather

CHAPTER 8

ADVENTURE

Life is one big adventure, and should be lived that way. The height and breath of that adventure is up to you. Refuse to settle for a boring, mundane and limited existence. You were born for greatness. You have the ability to do great things. Your life should be exciting. Expand who you are. Allow yourself to stretch beyond your previous limitations.

Think bigger thoughts. Explore the depths of your creativity. Reach for new levels. Do more and achieve more. Destroy the 'box' mentality that says, 'so far and no further.' Go ahead and attempt new and uncharted waters, or paths. You only have one life, so make it count. Do the things you have always wanted to do. What are you waiting for? You do not have all the time in the world. Use what you got.

Have you ever gone to bed, and could not wait for the morning to come? You were excited about something great that was happening in your life, or some future and momentous occasion. You were excited about the expected harvest of success from the 'dream seeds' that you had planted.

What comes to mind when you think of the word ADVENTURE? Adventure is defined as: *an unusual and exciting experience or activity.* It is also defined as: *a bold and risky, but yet exciting exploration of the unknown.* Adventure is: *doing what you have never done and going where you have never gone.*

Adventure does have an element of danger and surprise, but it also has an element of excitement, discovery, increase and paradigm shift. Men like Christopher Columbus, the Italian explorer and colonizer, were known for discovering or colonizing new lands. Colonization, though often viewed in a negative sense, did change the way certain nations thought or lived. This is an example of paradigm shift, where the usual way of thinking and living changes. Paradigm shifts happen because of scientific, political, spiritual and social revolutions, like The Industrial Revolution, Civil Rights Movement, and Religious Reformations.

Jesus is probably the greatest shifter of paradigm when it comes to religion and spirituality, as well as death and life. He created a huge shift in people living by tradition and cultural downloads to living by God's revelation about life, if they chose to accept it. He introduced Heaven's Kingdom culture. This Kingdom culture was designed to better the lives of people, as well as grant them deeper understanding of origin, purpose and destiny, and a place in Heaven.

An adventurous spirit allows you to explore paths and areas previously uncharted. That comes with its challenges—perhaps fear of the unknown—and adjustments to the new things that enter your life, thereby requiring you to adjust and change. Do not let anything intimidate you. Do not let circumstances bully you into submitting to a dull and restricted life. Mediocrity should have no place in your life.

You have to do more things that are meaningful and rewarding than just things that are convenient, but boring. God did not create you to live life in the shadows, but rather in the light. By being adventurous, you will forge new relationships, gain new skills and experiences. You will expand your world. You will definitely enrich your life.

Change requires a new way of thinking and executing those thoughts and ideas. Jesus said something interesting in the Bible. He said that no one puts a new patch on an old garment, for the new patch will cause a tear in the old. He then said that no one pours new wine into old wine skins, for they will burst (Matthew 9:16-17). Simply put, He was saying that to take on the new, the container has to be changed or renewed. It is pointless presenting new things to people who have adamantly decided they are not going to change. That is like putting new wine in an old wine skin. Trying to engage what you are not ready for can lead to further trouble or unnecessary discomfort or setback.

If you are waking up with no joy or excitement about your day, then make some changes. Change your thinking, change your outlook, change your attitude, and if you have to, change your career. Doing something you really hate, or something you find purposeless cannot bring you any joy . If you do what you love, you will love what you do. This is not to say that you will not have to do certain things that are less desirable. Nevertheless, use what you love as a motivation to tackle even the unsavoury tasks. Find things that will motivate you for the day ahead. If you are unenthusiastic about your life, you probably will not be excited about your dreams either.

In your heart, you desire more. There is always more in life for you. Do not just settle for what is. Average is not your aim. Remain expectant of great things to come. Be expectant that great things will happen in your life. Cast your gaze beyond the horizon. This means that you must not limit your thinking and understanding to your experiences and current knowledge. Make room for new things in your life. Allow yourself to be stretched. T. D. Jakes said: *"You may not always know what your 'more' is, but you desire it."*

To this I say, if you desire more, then pursue more. Satisfaction or contentment does not mean you do not need or crave more. You can still reach for more, while experiencing contentment. If you have reached a plateau, then build new hills of expectation, hope, and creativity. If you have reached the top of your mountain, then find a taller one to climb. Sky is the limit. Move up; go further; achieve more. In the gym, when I have reached my final rep and feel I cannot do another, I gather all my wit and strength and push another two or three reps. You can go beyond your norm or limits.

One must understand that great wealth does not always equal great success and purpose. I tend to shy away from things that are not fulfilling to my soul. Jaime Lyn Beatty said, *"Jobs fill your pocket; adventures fill your soul."* Many rich people are frustrated or bored with life, perhaps because they stopped being adventurous. When you decide that your wealth and comfort are all you need, you end up settling for a life that *fits in a fish bowl.* God wants you to live outside the box. God wants you thinking and acting bigger than you have been thinking or acting before. God does not want you to stay in the fish bowl, but to explore the vast oceans of possibilities.

Being adventurous nullifies a mundane and predictable life. It nullifies monotony. Embracing an adventurous life guarantees a greater life of discovery, excitement and fulfilment. It is all about launching out beyond the known, and beyond the present routines and habits. The apostle Peter, a fisherman by trade, got a taste of this when he obeyed Jesus by launching out into the deep sea and letting down his nets. Up until then, Peter and his companions had toiled all night, but had caught no fish. Now here was Jesus asking them to drop their nets in the day for a catch. These were experienced fishermen. They knew that fishing with nets was better at night, and nearly impossible in the day. They were exhausted from a fruitless night out at sea (Luke 5:4-10). They threw their nets back in the water probably just to humour Jesus.

To their surprise, they caught so many fish, the boat started to sink. They had to call in another boat to help with the catch. This catch of fish was an adventure that brought a great reward, and a great profit. It was a miraculous catch. Did they know this was going to be the result? No, but I am quite certain they were glad they took the adventure Jesus presented. Now, the adventure did not end there. They followed Jesus on a greater adventure of rescuing men's souls (Luke 5:10-11). Do not be afraid to go on adventures that present themselves to you. You may never know what major change and breakthrough they can bring.

Many people, who have been deflated, worn out and despondent, have returned from adventures with renewed energy, excitement and overhaul. Adventure can spark something fresh or new in you. ADVENTURE CAUSES YOU TO ABANDON THE OLD AND MONOTONOUS FOR THE NEW AND GLORIOUS!

I would hate you to grow old, and then look back over your life with disappointment because you missed adventurous opportunities. Take careful note of this quote I included by Huckleberry Finn author Mark Twain: *"Twenty years from now you will be more disappointed by the things that you didn't do than by the ones you did. So throw off the bowlines. Sail away from the safe harbour. Catch the trade winds in your sails. Explore—Dream—Discover."*

Treat each day, week or year as a new adventure. A new day can bring new friends, new thoughts, new ways, new awakenings, new energy, new paths and new ideas. You can go places in your mind or imagination, but do not let it end there. Take action; go for the experience. Get your *feet wet*.

People who live in the *comfortable centre* or *safe zone* do not get to experience the wondrous and adventurous things those experience who live on the edge. Peter in the Bible was the one who stepped out the boat and walked on water. The other disciples stayed safe in the boat, but they missed the wonderful, miraculous experience Jesus offered (Matthew 14:28-29). Christopher Columbus summed this up when he said, *"You can never cross the ocean until you have the courage to lose sight of the shore."*

Climbing up that huge mountain to get to the top is adventurous, but it will require work and dedication. The adventure is worth the sacrifice. Remember, mountains seem formidable and challenging, until you climb them and stand on top of them. Conquer your mountains, instead of letting them conquer you. You will never experience more by staying in the same place or thinking and acting in the exact same way as before.

Do not forget to have fun in life. Adventure should be thrilling. Go big on adventure. When you look back at what you have discovered, achieved or acquired, you will be pleasantly surprised. When you read about the lives of the many Bible heroes, you will be amazed at the adventurous lives they lived. Let us look at some of them:

> ➤ **Noah:** This man was living a fairly mundane life until God interrupted his normality. When God offered him an adventure, Noah accepted, even though he was now dealing with a God who was greater than anything, and had a mandate that was out of this world. In fact, the task He set Noah—and more particular, Noah's obedience to fulfil it—probably caused his contemporaries to question Noah's sanity. God called Noah to BUILD AN ARK.

It had never rained before. Back then, the earth had been watered by a mist and water from the ground (Genesis 2). Why did God call Noah to build a big boat? The Bible lets us know that Noah was a righteous man and walked with God (Genesis 6). God wanted to preserve him and his family—just eight people out of Earth's entire population, utterly lost in their sin. Ultimately, Noah prepared for this adventure by building the Ark for many years, while preaching to his calloused generation to repent from wickedness. I am quite sure many mocked and laughed at him. Eventually, Noah and his family and selected animals survived the damning Flood that wiped out all people and living creatures (Genesis 7).

➢ **Abraham:** In Genesis 12, God invited Abraham on a daring and exciting adventure, telling him to leave his home country and venture to a different land. God promised to bless him and give him numerous descendants, even though he was childless. You can read about the amazing accomplishments of Abraham's adventure from Genesis 13 to 25. He experienced new places and new friends, overcame enemies, and had his promised son Isaac when he was ninety-nine years old. Having a child at fifty or sixty would be quite an adventure; but to have one at nearly one-hundred is off the scale; it is adventure at its peak.

➢ **Joseph:** Joseph's adventure started with his dreams (Genesis 37). His brothers opposed him because of his dreams. They threw him in a pit, and then sold him as a slave. He ended up in a foreign country called Egypt. He worked for Potiphar who was an officer of Pharaoh. Even though Joseph was experiencing adverse circumstances God was with him, and God prospered him and blessed him (Genesis 39).

Potiphar ended up putting Joseph in charge of his household. The adventure continued when Potiphar's wife made sexual advances towards Joseph. She wanted him to sleep with her. Joseph refused because of his integrity and fear (respect) of the Lord. Potiphar's wife then made false accusations against him, accusing him of trying to rape her

(Genesis 39). Joseph then found himself in prison. Talk about an adventure gone wrong. How low could one go, yet remain optimistic?

Yet even in prison, God favoured Joseph. He ended up interpreting the dreams of two men in prison. After two years one of those men informed Pharaoh of his ability to interpret dreams. Pharaoh called for Joseph to interpret his dreams. Suddenly things changed for Joseph. He went from prisoner to Prime Minister of Egypt. Pharaoh recognised the wisdom of God in him. Joseph practically gave Pharaoh a plan on how to save Egypt from a severe famine. Let me quote to you what Pharaoh said:

"Then Pharaoh said to Joseph, 'Inasmuch as God has shown you all this, there is no one as discerning and wise as you. You shall be over my house, and all my people shall be ruled according to your word; only in regard to the throne will I be greater than you.' And Pharaoh said to Joseph, 'See, I have set you over all the land of Egypt'" (Genesis 41:39-41, NKJV).

➤ **Moses:** Moses had quite an adventurous life from birth. His mother hid him in the river Nile in a waterproof basket. The government of Egypt was slaughtering male babies to keep the Israelite population from multiplying greatly. Pharaoh's daughter found Moses and she kept him as her own. Pharaoh's daughter unknowingly called on Moses' very own mother to nurse him for her. A Hebrew baby grew up in the palace instead of being dead in a grave, or cast among the Hebrew slaves (Exodus 2).

When Moses became a man and learned of the sufferings of his people, it affected him. He ended up killing an Egyptian for beating up a Hebrew slave. Moses then fled for his life after Pharaoh put a bounty on his head.

Whilst in exile, he met Jethro, and married one of his daughters, Zipporah. The adventure got more exciting and daring when God called Moses to return to Egypt and rescue all the enslaved Hebrews. This was a very daunting task, but God promised Moses He would be with him and empower him (Exodus 3). Moses reluctantly accepted the adventure. God then did many amazing miraculous things through Moses. These included:

> the ten plagues that ruined Egypt
> the parting of the Red Sea
> the provision of manna from Heaven and quail for food for all the Israelites
> water flowing from a dry rock.

> **King David:** David's adventurous life began when he was a young boy in his early teens. Out in the field minding the sheep, he encountered a lion and a bear on different occasions. He killed them both in order to protect the sheep. As a teenager, I probably would have taken off running to save my own life. There was no great crowd of people to applaud David's victories.

The adventure continued when the prophet Samuel anointed David as the future king of Israel. God bypassed all seven of David's brothers and chose him, the 'runt' of the family. This historical account is found in 1 and 2 Samuel, and in 1 and 2 Chronicles.

David encountered more adventure where he confronted Goliath, a giant and an intimidating enemy of the Israelites.

After killing this giant, King Saul offered David a position in his army as a commander. He did well and quickly rose to the top and became renowned. Adventure took a downturn when King Saul tried to kill him out of jealousy. David fled for his life. Sometimes great victories can bring you new enemies, not just supporters. You cannot paddle a boat and not make waves.

When the dust settled, David still stood strong and eventually became king. At this point, his adventure peaked. Throughout his journey, he displayed his wonderful skill as a valiant warrior, psalmist and writer. He was a solid and fearless king, yet tender-hearted toward God, and an avid worshipper.

> **Paul, the Apostle:** Paul, formally known as Saul had a bleak and dark start to his adventure. For starters, he was well known for persecuting Christians, dragging them to prison, and approvingly bearing witnessed to their execution by stoning. He thought he was doing God a favour. His adventure took a drastic turn when he encountered a manifestation of the ascended Jesus, and his life was never the same again (Acts 9).

Saul was renamed Paul. His previous life of opposing Christians turned into one of preaching the same Gospel message they preached. He became a supporter of the people he initially hated and persecuted. He was willing to endure suffering and death threats for the Gospel's sake. Paul went on to write more than half of the New Testament of the Bible. He also became a spiritual mentor to those under his care, particularly Timothy and Titus. He was willing to give up his life for the sake of the Gospel.

> **Jesus Christ:** Jesus' adventure began in a miraculous way. He was born without the intervention of a natural father. It is called the virgin birth (Matthew 1:18-25). Jesus was the only man to walk perfectly on the earth (Hebrews 4:15). He was God in flesh.

The Bible records that Jesus grew in wisdom, statue and favour with God and man. He claimed to be God. He performed many great miracles, like raising the dead, healing sick bodies and walking on water. He fed multitudes with a single meal. He displayed great compassion towards the disadvantaged ones.

Finally, he endured a cruel punishment and crucifixion on a cross for the whole world (Hebrews 12:2). He did it so that people could have a place in Heaven. His life was short-lived (lasting approximately thirty-three years), yet He accomplished some extraordinary things. What an adventure! This adventure brought people close to God. It gave people access to God (Ephesians 2:18). It showed that God cared for the human race, and continues to do so.

If you believe in life after death, then you know that adventure does not end in death. God has more in the 'after-life.' In Scripture, God gives people a glimpse of this; like a sneak preview (John 14:2; Revelations 21). It will get even more exciting and glorious. Are you ready for it?

The moment you realise your dream, you know there is more adventure in store; buckets of blessing, triumph and paradigm shifts awaiting you. Follow your dreams and let them lead you through more doors of great adventure.

"STARTING STRONG
IS GOOD. FINISHING
STRONG IS EPIC."

-Robin Sharma

CHAPTER 9

FINISHING WELL

Finishing well stems from the desire to see what you started arrive at its full and successful end or finish. Starting something does not guarantee success, but finishing does.

We all want a good start in life. However, we must also desire a good finish, meaning we must be prepared to put in the effort. We must be prepared to deal with the obstacles or turbulences life brings.

You have a dream? Well, that is good. You want to start your dream? Well, that is even better. You want to see the fulfilment of your dream? Well, that is superb. When I thought of writing this book, I began to develop the concepts. I saw a finished book, even though I had not started to type it yet. You would not be reading this book had I not started, and most importantly, persevered until I'd finished it.

As I meditated, researched and wrote, drawing from life in general, and my own life story, the book began to take shape. I wanted a product that was vivid, inspiring, educational, and life changing. I believe, after writing for approximately three years, I have successfully achieved my goal. Those who have had a chance to pre-read my manuscript have had amazing responses and reviews. I am certain you too, my dear reader, have already been impacted by this book.

There will never be a finish without a start. Equally, a start is pointless without an end in mind. Why even start if you cannot commit to finishing? You have a dream, you need to see it through to the end. I have the ability to juggle several projects simultaneously. I am very dedicated with my projects. I put in the time and work. Success is not a friend of laziness. Lazy people hardly finish or accomplish anything great.

An aeroplane does not take off unless there is a flight plan and a destination or landing point. There is purpose attached to starting. The start must lead somewhere. An aeroplane that taxies down the runway and takes off into the sky constitutes a successful start. However, during the flight, there may be turbulences and other complications. When you have started to live your dreams, there will be challenges and obstacles. Buckle up and stay in your seat. Hold your position. Turbulences will not last forever. They are a momentary discomfort during flights. Even though emergency landings are necessary, do not keep on landing your dreams prematurely at the sight of every difficulty or trouble. Too many stops or interruptions may prolong your finish.

In 1912, Jim Thorpe, a Native American had his running shoes stolen on the morning of his Olympic track and field events. Instead of complaining and giving up, he found a mismatched pair of shoes in the trash and ran in them to win two Olympic gold medals that day. They stole his shoes but not his dream and his passion and determination to finish and win.

Starting gives you a sense of what is possible and the excitement of what could be achieved. Finishing gives you a sense of fulfilment and builds confidence and passion for the next dream or project. However, there is grace and understanding, especially when circumstances beyond your control hamper your finish. Do not wallow in sadness and guilt. Reset and restart, if possible.

The Covid-19 pandemic, along with all the restrictions and lockdowns, has left many people fatigued, and even depressed. Many struggled through it. Many lost precious family members. We all were affected in some way, shape, or form. We all wanted to get through it and see it end. We all wanted to get on with life. We all wanted to overcome it. As humans, we have tenacity and resilience, even when bombarded by adversity. We fight back and we overcome. For those of us who are much stronger, let us be strong for those who need strength to live their lives and fulfil their dreams again.

On the flip side, the lockdowns invited many of us to pause, rest, and re-evaluate what we had considered to be important in life, especially the things we take for granted. People developed new and creative ways of doing things. Strangers became our friends. Neighbours connected more. Generosity took on new forms. Love and the true spirit of humanity became evident. The world can be such a cold and divided place. Nevertheless, I believe unity is alive and growing. We are better together than apart.

Running towards our destiny is like a relay race. There are supporters to help us get our dreams to the finish line. They will cheer you on, inspiring you to cross the finish line.

What you finish may very well be the catalyst for someone else's start. At the start of a year, many businesses, organizations, or schools put into practice what they'd planned for the new year. Some things have to be planned in advance before they can be executed. I recently spent four weeks decorating a newly built house for a friend of mine. As my team and I worked, it was quite evident that much planning had gone into the building. There was land surveying, planning permission, architectural plans and designs, inspections, along with all the tradesmen to bring it to a finish. The house looks amazing because it was well thought out. If you do not plan well, you might not end up building well, which jeopardizes finishing well.

Take time to pause and review your dream journey or the goals you've set. Stay positive and do not be too hard on yourself. Get help when you need it. Do not try to be a lone ranger. Pay attention to the details and process, but also keep your eye on the prize. That will keep you motivated.

If you are not passionate about the project you are working on, you might be tempted to quit before completion, so take on things you really love to do. Track your progress. Give yourself moments to enjoy your progress. Rewards along the way will spur you on to the finish line, especially with projects that have a long process before completion.

In closing, the Bible says that the end of a thing is better than its start (Ecclesiastes 7:8). You will be remembered more for what and how you finished than what and how you started. Aim to finish well.

DREAMS ARE A DOOR
INTO YOUR FUTURE. DO
NOT IGNORE THEM.

- Aubrey Morris

CHAPTER 10

REFLECTION

Where are you in life? What season do you find yourself in? What choices have you made, and where have they lead you? What do you want to change? How do you need to reposition yourself in order to take advantage of new opportunities? These are important questions to ask yourself from time to time. Re-evaluate your life journey. Take stock of your life regularly. Do not just let life happen, but make life happen.

Are you satisfied? Are you happy? Are you at peace? Do you want more? Some people reach their end even before they arrive there. In other words, they have given up. They are just coasting towards the end, frazzled and demotivated. They want less, and not more. They are at the quitting stage. My prayer is that you find such people and help them ignite passion and purpose again. Place this book in their hand. Give them a taste for the better and greater. Give them this road map that will guide them in living a full life. Help them realize that the adventure is not over yet. Share your highs and lows with them. Let them see that they are not alone. Let them see that 'more' is possible.

Keep your dreams alive. They should be the reason you wake up in the morning. You will succeed, and your success will inspire others to succeed. Maybe you have been holding back.

Now it is time to unleash more of who you are, and what you can create.

I know you have been dreaming; now dream more and achieve more. Purpose and destiny await you. I am glad you have read this book. My passion is to see many people live extravagantly, dream extravagantly and achieve extravagantly. It is time to rethink and reshape your life.

Look at the questions on the next page, and answer them as honestly as you can. Remember, I am praying for you, and I am rooting for your success. Think of yourself as being on the racetrack with a great crowd of supporters cheering you on to success. Go ahead and do what you know to do. Do what you need to do. Do what you want to do. Live a full satisfied and purposeful life. Dream on!

REFLECTIVE QUESTIONS

1. How has this book inspired you?

_____

_____

_____

_____

_____

_____

_____

2. What are some of the dreams you have, and what steps have you taken to achieve them?

_____

_____

_____

_____

_____

_____

_____

3. What are some of the challenges you face, and what are you
    doing to overcome them?

_____

_____

_____

_____

_____

_____

4. What are you doing to nurture and protect your dreams?

_____

_____

_____

_____

_____

_____

_____

5. Who are some of your heroes or heroines, and how do they inspire you?

_____

_____

_____

_____

_____

_____

_____

MORE ABOUT THE AUTHOR

Aubrey Morris was born in Durban, South Africa. After high school, he attended Edgewood University where he graduated as an Educator. He taught in two schools in South Africa over a period of 8 years, and then immigrated to Ireland where he taught for 10 years. In South Africa, he founded the Addington Youth Club (A.C.C); ran Choir and Drama groups through which he inspired the youth. He also developed his musical abilities, performing in concerts and church services. He immigrated to Ireland in 2005, where he continued to teach and serve as a youth worker, while attending studies in Theology. He has grown into a seasoned teacher, preacher, motivational speaker and musician.

He has also been involved with community organizations like NEWRY FOOD BANK, SOSAD, CONCERN and SPIRIT RADIO. He also oversaw a Men's Group called MOMENTUM.

Aubrey also served on the WAKEUP board, a youth building organization in Ireland, as well as co-supervising the WAKEUP MUSIC BAND. He also facilitated mission trips to Southern Africa. Aubrey has also pursued studies in film making and acting. Aubrey is also the owner of Morris Painting & Deco business.

Aubrey is married to Auriel Morris. They have two sons: Dillon and Levi. The family resides in Ireland.

Other books by Aubrey Morris:

"THE POTENTIAL OF YOUR LIFE"

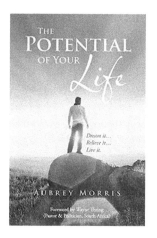

"Potential of Your Life" is a motivational book loaded with spiritual and practical insight to equip you and leave you passionate about life, as you exercise your potential and live out your God-given purpose. It will help bring out the best in you, as you discover your significance.

Available: *wherever books are sold.*

"WISDOM FOR LIFE 101"

Wisdom for Life 101 comprises 101 bite-size messages on WISDOM, the MAIN thing in life. Wisdom is the seedbed from which we cultivate an effective, wholesome and meaningful life.

Available: *wherever books are sold.*

"WHY IS GOD SO GOOD?"

Why Is God So Good? seeks to take you on a pleasant journey on the topic of God's absolute goodness and love for humankind. It explores God's father-heart and character that truly benefits our lives.

Available: *wherever books are sold.*

Lightning Source UK Ltd.
Milton Keynes UK
UKHW021826251022
411083UK00003B/40/J